ARIZONA
A Short History   by Odie B. Faulk

By Odie B. Faulk

Tom Green: A Fightin' Texan (Waco, 1963)
The Last Years of Spanish Texas, 1778–1821 (The Hague, 1964)
Texas After Spindletop (Austin, 1965)
Arizona's State Historical Society (Tucson, 1966)
John Baptist Salpointe: Soldier of the Cross (Tucson, 1966)
John Robert Baylor: Confederate Governor of Arizona (Tucson, 1966)
The Constitution of Occidente (Tucson, 1967)
Too Far North—Too Far South (Los Angeles, 1967)
Land of Many Frontiers (New York, 1968)
The Geronimo Campaign (New York, 1969)
Arizona: A Short History (Norman, 1970)

Co-authored:

Lancers for the King (Phoenix, 1965)
A Successful Failure (Austin, 1965)

Library of Congress Catalog Card Number: 75-108808

ISBN: 0–8061–1222–0

FOR NANCY:
a native Arizonan, and
FOR LAURA AND RICHARD:
five-year residents

PREFACE

Casual visitors, tourists, and even a few native residents sometimes comment that Nature discriminated against Arizona. They view its 113,909 square miles as a harsh, inhospitable land of cactus, sagebrush, and tumbleweeds, of too much heat and too little rain. Yet the state is incredibly blessed. It is a land rich in geography, containing mountains and valleys, lakes and deserts, towering pines as well as thorny cacti, lush vegetation as well as rolling sand dunes. It ranges from 139 feet above sea level near Yuma to towering peaks that soar more than 13,000 feet.

Its climate varies from almost perpetual snow to hot desert where the thermometer climbs at times above the 120-degree mark. It has summer resort areas as well as well-known attractions for winter visitors; sand buggies race within fifty miles of ski facilities—and both operate simultaneously. Almost one-fourth of the state is National Forest, while cacti such as the saguaro and the organ pipe are commemorated by National Monuments.

Arizona also is a land rich in people, including Indians, Latin Americans, Negroes, Orientals, and Anglo-Americans. Just as its geography ranges from the pleasant and mild to the harsh and inhospitable, so its people vary from good to bad and in between. Here have been performed deeds of daring, of dishonor, of valor, of dishonesty. And it is a land rich in past, present, and future, with a history stretching back three-quarters of a century before the landing of the celebrated English settlers of the Eastern seaboard, and a future bright with promise.

This volume is intended as an introduction to the harsh, varied, beautiful land that is Arizona. It is not intended as a scholarly treatise that opens new avenues of research, but rather as a summary, a synthesis of the 400-plus years of the state's past, a look at the present, and an overview of its potential in readable terms. I hope the newcomer, the winter visitor, the tourist, and the student will find it a ready source of information for the sweep, the color, and the pageantry of Arizona history, while the long-time resident will discover new reasons for loving his state. Approximately one-fourth of the book is related to the Spanish-Mexican years and another one-fourth to the years since statehood, leaving half the book devoted to the territorial epoch. While there is room for debate about this proportioning, I feel that the period between 1863 and

1912, the territorial years, is the most important formative period in the shaping of the Arizona of today, and thus it is emphasized in order to give the reader a better understanding of Arizona as it now is.

In drafting the present work, I have incurred numerous debts. During my five years' residence in Arizona, I taught a university-level course in Arizona history in Tucson, Fort Huachuca, Phoenix, Pinetop-Showlow, and Yuma; to the hundreds of students who took that course I am obligated for criticism and comment that gave me a better understanding of the state. Many scholars in the state aided my quest for facts, such as Bert Fireman of the Arizona Historical Foundation; Mrs. Marguerite B. Cooley of the Department of Library and Archives; Don Phillips and James Murphy of the Arizona Pioneers' Historical Society; Richard Yates of Arizona Western College Library; and John A. Carroll of the University of Arizona. I also wish specifically to thank the Oklahoma State University Research Foundation for providing funds that enabled me to complete parts of the work, and the Oklahoma State University Library for generous co-operation. Don Bufkin of Tucson, who provided the maps, has done me so many favors over the years that I can never repay him; similarly, Librarian Margaret Sparks and Archivist Charles Colley of the Arizona Pioneers' Historical Society aided my search for pictures. And I owe a great debt to the friends and scholars in Arizona who have read the manuscript and offered comment: Andrew Wallace of Northern Arizona University; Harwood P. Hinton of the University of Arizona; Sidney B. Brinckerhoff, director of the Arizona Pioneers' Historical Society; and others. The members of the staff of the University of Oklahoma Press have my lasting gratitude for their generous assistance in producing this book.

Finally I note with pride that my daughter, Nancy Marie, was born at St. Joseph's Hospital in Tucson on August 15, 1963, making her a native Arizonan. This book is dedicated to her, to my wife Laura, and my son Richard in memory of our five years in "The Grand Canyon State."

ODIE B. FAULK

CONTENTS

Arizona: A Short History

PART II: *The Territorial Years*

PART III: *The Statehood Years*

ILLUSTRATIONS

xiii

Following page 114

First Territorial Officials of Arizona
The Steamer *Gila* on the Colorado River
Train Arriving at Benson in the 1890's
Pipe Springs National Monument
Lieutenant Charles B. Gatewood
"El Potrero," Home of Pete Kitchen
The Sierra Bonita Ranch
Logging Near Flagstaff in the 1890's

Following page 178

Tombstone Courthouse
Lynching of James Heith
John H. Slaughter
A "Zanjero"
Phoenix in 1891
President Taft Signs the Arizona Statehood Bill, 1912
George W. P. Hunt
"Operation Haylift," 1967

MAPS

ARIZONA: A Short History

Part One: **THE COLONIAL YEARS**

THE AGE OF DISCOVERY AND EXPLORATION

Shortly after Easter Sunday, 1539, Fray Marcos de Niza was resting at Vacapa, an Indian village in central Sonora some two hundred miles south of the present southern boundary of Arizona. A Franciscan monk, he had no European companions, just a few friendly Indians who had come north with him, far beyond the rim of Spanish settlement. Suddenly a small group of Indians came over the horizon from the north and made their way laboriously to the little village. They were burdened "with a very large cross, as tall as a man," Fray Marcos later reported. The sight of that cross brought him great joy and excitement—but not solely for religious reasons. That cross symbolized great wealth to the north, in the land that would be called Arizona, and it led directly to the first penetration and exploration of that area by Europeans.

Fray Marcos was marching northward at the orders of the viceroy of New Spain (as Mexico was then called), Antonio de Mendoza, in search of seven reportedly wealthy cities, the legendary Seven Cities of Cíbola. Spanish tradition held that seven bishops had fled Spain centuries before, during the Moorish invasion, and had each founded a Christian city in a distant land. Then, in 1527, at the northwestern edge of settlement in New Spain, an Indian named Tejo (or Tejoc) had been captured; he told of seven wondrous cities to the north, cities of great wealth. Finally, in 1536, four survivors of shipwreck on Galveston Island had been found near Culiacán, in present Sinaloa. Their leader, Álvar Núñez Cabeza de Vaca, told Viceroy Mendoza that they had seen no evidence of great wealth in their trek from Texas westward, but that they had heard from Indians of seven rich cities somewhere to the north. Mendoza tried to persuade Cabeza de Vaca to lead an expedition north to conquer these cities, but Cabeza de Vaca declined, as did two of the others. The fourth, however, a Negro slave named Estebán (or Estebanico), was acquired by the viceroy and in 1539 was sent as guide to Fray Marcos. Theirs was to be a preliminary reconnaissance, to be followed by a full-scale expedition if they should actually locate the golden cities. The viceroy's instructions to Fray Marcos were broad: to gather information about the native tribes, the nature and fertility of the land, the course of rivers, and, especially, to seek knowledge of "the rocks and metals. And of whatever objects it may be possible to bring or send samples, bring or send them, in order that his majesty be informed of everything." Above all, however, he was to look for large cities, word of which, if found, was to be communicated "with due secrecy."

Fray Marcos departed Culiacán, the last outpost, on March 7, 1539, guided by Esteban and accompanied by approximately twenty friendly Indians from farther south. Arriving at Vacapa, Fray Marcos was welcomed by the Indians, and there he stopped to rest. There also he sent Esteban ahead to scout the countryside; should he find anything, he was to report it by means of a cross to be carried by Indian messengers: "In case the discovery was of medium importance, he was to send me a cross of one span in length; if important, the cross was to be two spans in length; and if more important than New Spain, he should send me a large cross." Four days later messengers arrived with a cross as large as a man, which, understandably, excited Fray Marcos. Following in Esteban's footsteps, the Franciscan marched northward, probably following the Sonora River. He never caught up with Esteban, however; the Negro always kept advancing, leaving large crosses behind to guide Fray Marcos. Near the headwaters of the Sonora River, Esteban, and after him Fray Marcos, went almost due north to the upper reaches of the San Pedro River, following it into Arizona. Ironically the great silver lode later discovered at Tombstone lay beneath their feet as they trod the banks of the San Pedro northward into the area, but they passed it by in ignorance.

Moving north and slightly to the east, they went near the present town of Benson, crossed the White Mountains, and arrived at the high desert country in northeastern Arizona, near the New Mexican border. There, on May 31, Fray Marcos was surprised to meet one of the Indians who had been with Estebán—and the Indian brought news of disaster. Estebán and his following had approached the first of the Seven Cities. The inhabitants had warned them not to enter, but Estebán insisted. The inhabitants of the city placed him and his followers in a large house outside the city, took all their possessions from them, and gave them neither food nor water. The next morning the inhabitants of the city fell on Estebán and his party, killing most of them. A few escaped, one of whom happened to meet Fray Marcos and tell the sad tale. The missionary feared for his life, for the Indians with him were friends and relatives of those killed with Estebán. To persuade the terrified Indians to accompany him farther, the Franciscan gave them all the trinkets in his possession, gifts he had been bringing to Cíbola. They agreed, but sullenly and after repeatedly threatening his life.

Thus guided, he was brought to a hill from which he could observe the first of the Seven Cities, which, the Indians informed him, was the smallest of the seven. "The houses are . . . all of stone, with their stories and flat roofs," he later reported. "As far as I could see from a height where I placed myself to observe, the settlement is larger than the city of Mexico." He stated that he wished to go closer to the city to observe, "But finally I feared, considering the danger, and that if I should die there would be no knowledge of this land which, in my estimation, is the largest and best of all yet discovered." He contented himself by making a mound of stones and placing a small wooden cross atop it, claiming the land for Spain and naming it the "New Kingdom of Saint Francis." Then he commenced his return trip, as he declared, "with much more fear than food." By September he was in Mexico City to make his report to the viceroy.

Fray Marcos' report had an electrifying effect. Soon the whole population of Mexico City had heard of the large cities to the north, cities actually viewed by the viceroy's exploratory party. Speculation centered around who would command the major expedition to conquer these cities—and reap the rumored rich treasure to be had there. This speculation ended with the appointment of Francisco Vásquez de Coronado. Born in 1510 in Salamanca, Spain, Coronado had come to the New World with Viceroy Mendoza, and, in 1539, was serving as governor of Nueva Galicia, New Spain's northwestern province which extended northward indefinitely. Young men rushed to join the expedition, expecting to share in the rich booty. The major portion of the cost of outfitting the expedition was borne by Mendoza and Coronado; the remainder came from some of the recruits. Had the funds come from the royal treasury, the proceeds would have had to be deposited there. As a private venture, only the royal *quinto* (a tax of 20 per cent) would go to the king.

On February 23, 1540, Mendoza reviewed the departing expedition at Compostela. Behind Coronado rode 336 Spaniards, followed by almost 1,000 Indian allies, and behind them came some 1,500 horses and mules, plus numberless cattle and sheep. Moving along the coast, with orders to lend naval support in the conquest of the Seven Cities, were two vessels under the command of Captain Hernando de Alarcón. The trek to Culiacán from Compostela provided a "shakedown" for the members of the northward-bound party. On April 22 this last Spanish outpost was left behind, and, guided by Fray Marcos, the Spaniards and their allies marched northward on their journey of conquest. They crossed into Arizona following the same route that Fray Marcos had used—the valley of the San Pedro, across the White Mountains, and the high desert of northeastern Arizona.

On July 7, 1540, the army reached its goal, the golden city viewed by Fray Marcos. Smoke signals could be seen rising from various places in the vicinity, and two to three hundred defenders were drawn up in battle formation outside, blowing horns and making hostile gestures. Coronado tried to explain through an interpreter that he came in peace to defend them in the name of the Spanish king. When the Indian defenders tried to kill the interpreter, Coronado ordered the charge. Twice the Indians attacked, reinforced by more warriors who had been hidden inside the pueblo. The Spaniards kept pressing forward, however —hunger drove them on. Their supplies were exhausted, and they knew the only way to get something to eat was to reduce the city to surrender. Courage had little to do with the outcome, for both sides had a sufficiency of that commodity; it was Spanish firearms, horses, and military precision which turned the tide of battle in their favor. When the Indians indicated a desire for terms, the Spaniards hurried inside to eat.

Coronado learned in a council with the Indian chieftains that what he had captured was a Zuñi Indian pueblo named Hawikúh. In the vicinity were five other pueblos, bringing the total to six—not seven—cities. Nor were they filled with gold or silver. On August 3, Coronado sent a letter to Viceroy Mendoza, stating angrily, "Fray Marcos has not told the truth in a single thing that he said, except the name of the cities and the large stone houses." Fray Marcos himself bore the message to the viceroy. But the search for treasure in the north country was not over. Coronado still hoped to find quick riches in the form of gold or silver in the possession of some Indian civilization.

Major Indian tribes of Arizona. *Drawn by Don Bufkin*

Therefore samples of precious metals, jewels, and pearls were shown to the Zuñis with questions about where such might be had. The Indians were quick to realize that the Spanish quest for such baubles might be their deliverance, and stated that such could be had to the west in the kingdoms of Tontonteac and Tusayán. Coronado immediately dispatched Captain Pedro de Tovar with seventeen mounted men to investigate. Passing through the petrified forest, Tovar arrived at Hopi Indian villages. A battle followed, but the Hopis had no real heart for fighting the Spaniards. They already had heard of the arrival of these ferocious men "riding about on animals that devoured people" [horses]. The other Hopi pueblos likewise surrendered, and were shown samples of precious metals. And they, like the Zuñis, pointed west; Tovar's report to Coronado stressed that "notice was had of a great river where people lived who possessed wealth."

To investigate this report, Coronado sent twenty-five men under the command of Captain García López de Cárdenas. Leaving Hawikúh late in August, Cárdenas led his party west along Tovar's trail to the Hopi villages, then marched across present northern Arizona. Unexpectedly they came to the edge of a canyon "from whose brink it looked as if to the opposite side it must be more than three or four leagues." Cárdenas had discovered the Grand Canyon, but he was not impressed. He was seeking gold, not natural wonders. After three fruitless days' search for some way to descend to the river they could see a mile below, the Spaniards returned to Hawikúh to make their report of failure.

Coronado did not realize that the river which Cárdenas reported having seen was, at the time, being visited by the naval arm of his expedition—but several hundred miles downstream. Alarcón sailed his ships up the Colorado as far as he dared go, then took to the longboats and proceeded upriver. Possibly he reached the mouth of the Gila (and thus present Arizona), although his report made no mention of identifiable landmarks which would place him that far north. From natives in that region he heard of Fray Marcos' visit and of Coronado's arrival at the Seven Cities of Cíbola. Realizing that he could not lend naval support to Coronado, as his orders directed, Alarcón returned to Mexico after burying letters at the base of a tree and carving a suitable inscription on the trunk.

These letters were found by still another part of the Coronado expedition late in September. As Coronado had traveled north through present Sonora, he had ordered twenty-five men, commanded by Captain Melchior Díaz, to angle to the northwest and make contact with Alarcón. Coronado realized that his route was carrying him away from the coast and that he could expect no help from that direction. From the Sonora River Valley, Díaz moved through country controlled by Pima and Papago Indians, then turned almost due west, paralleling the present international boundary between Arizona and Sonora, a region so desolate that it later would be called *el Camino del Diablo* (the Devil's Highway). They arrived on the banks of the Colorado some eighty miles north of its mouth (about the present San Luis, Arizona). From the Yuma Indians, Díaz learned that Alarcón had been there and had departed. And he was led to a tree where he found a carved inscription stating: "Alarcón came this far. There are letters at the foot of this tree." The letters told of the naval captain's arrival, his wait, and his return to Mexico. Díaz and his men spent some time exploring in the vicinity, crossing the Colorado and seeing part of present California. However, Díaz accidentally impaled himself on his own lance and died, and his men returned to Culiacán after sending runners northward to make a full report to Coronado.

These messengers found the general and his expedition gone from Hawikúh. They had transferred their attention to the Río Grande valley at the invitation of Pueblo Indians there. They wintered in the vicinity of the present Albuquerque, searching for precious metals and suppressing rebellions by their hosts, who were surprised that the Spaniards were short of supplies and living off the Indians. These New Mexican natives likewise said that wealth could be found elsewhere to get their visitors to move on. In fact, these Pueblo Indians in New Mexico had one of their slaves, a plains native, spin a tale of a wondrous place where the rudest peasant ate from golden plates, a fabulous land called the Gran Quivira. In the spring of 1541, Coronado and part of his men, guided by this glib plains native, left New Mexico and crossed the Texas and Oklahoma Panhandles, eventually reaching a miserable village of mud and straw huts in central Kansas (near present Wichita). The only metal in the village was a copper amulet, probably of meteoric origin, worn by the chieftain. Under questioning the guide admitted that he had lied at the insistence of the Pueblo Indians. His task, he said, was to lead the Spaniards to the High Plains and get them lost (the New Mexican Indians did not know the function of the compass, which the Spaniards possessed). The guide was strangled, and the Spaniards returned in dejection to winter again at the New Mexican pueblos. Then, in the spring of 1542, Coronado ordered the return march to begin.

The general made his way to Mexico City as fast as

possible, where he made his report to Viceroy Mendoza. He had found no gold, no silver, no jewels, no pearls— only Indians willing to fight for their meager supplies of food. After a few months' rest, Coronado returned to his post as governor of Nueva Galicia. But his health had been ruined by the two years in the saddle, and much of his fortune was gone, for he had invested heavily in his ill-fated expedition. Then charges were brought against him by discontented investors, charges of mismanagement, of cruelty to the natives, even of having found wealth and concealing the knowledge for his own benefit. He was convicted, removed as governor, fined, and stripped of his titles. In 1546, however, a reviewing board in Spain absolved Coronado of the charges, but he died soon afterward. His report had a lingering influence on Arizona history, for it showed that in this region there was nothing that would attract Spaniards, no precious metals and no Indians to be easily exploited. Forty years would pass before another expedition penetrated that far north. The Coronado National Monument and Coronado National Forest commemorate this conquistador and perpetuate his memory today.

RETURN OF THE EUROPEANS

The epic voyage of Francis Drake, made in the years 1578–80, turned Spanish thoughts to the north country once again. Drake had raided boldly up the west coast of South and Central America, plundering Spain's treasure vessels and rich port cities; then, after pausing to rest and refit his ship in California, he circumnavigated the world, reaching England, where he was knighted for his deeds. The Spaniards could not believe that he had crossed the vast Pacific or dared the tempestuous Cape of Good Hope off South

Africa. They also knew he had not returned by way of the Straits of Magellan, for this route had been closely watched to intercept him. Therefore, the Spaniards concluded that Drake had returned by way of the long-sought Northwest Passage, a fabled water route around North America. So certain were they that this passage existed that they had given it a name: the Straits of Anián. And this passage was of such strategic value that the viceroy received orders from Madrid to begin a search for it.

Once again Franciscan missionaries were enlisted as explorers. The route chosen for the preliminary reconnaissance was down the Conchos River of northern Mexico, which flows into the Río Grande at the present Presidio, Texas; from there the party would venture northward by way of the Río Grande itself. This route was chosen because slave-catching expeditions in search of Indians had already penetrated as far as the Río Grande and even beyond, and had heard of pueblo tribes to the north. In this preliminary party were three missionaries, led by Fray Agustín Rodríguez, nine soldiers, and sixteen Indian servants. Setting out on June 5, 1581, the expedition soon arrived in the Pueblo country of New Mexico. The natives had forgotten their differences with Coronado and welcomed the Spaniards in friendly fashion. However, they soon proved their fickle nature when one priest decided to return to Mexico to make a report. Shortly after he separated himself from the main party, he was killed. Soon the soldiers and Indian allies decided to return to Mexico, but Rodríguez and his Franciscan companion determined to remain.

The report given by these soldiers stressed that no water route had been found, but that large numbers of Indians in New Mexico could easily be brought under Spanish domination. This report would be forwarded from Mexico

City to Madrid, where the king's advisers would study it and make recommendations, a process that was very slow. In the meantime, Franciscans in New Spain grew worried about their two brethren still in New Mexico and petitioned to send a rescue party. A wealthy Mexican miner, Antonio de Espejo, volunteered to raise an escort of troops at personal expense to accompany the friars, and the viceroy agreed to the project. Fray Bernadino Beltrán was placed in charge, and on November 10, 1582, the Beltrán-Espejo expedition set out down the Conchos River. Using the same route as the Rodríguez party had followed, they soon arrived in New Mexico to discover that the two padres had been martyred by the natives.

Espejo then revealed his true reasons for going north: he wanted to search for the Seven Cities and the Gran Quivira. A short trip eastward convinced him that little possibility of wealth existed on the High Plains, and so the expedition set out westward from the Río Grande. They arrived at Hawikúh on March 15 and remained there until April 7, listening eagerly to the Indians' tales of Coronado and collecting Indian blankets. Espejo and nine of his men ventured on westward to the Hopi villages attacked by Pedro de Tovar more than four decades earlier. Then the captain, with four of his men, journeyed on to a river they called Río de las Reyes (probably the Verde River). There they found mines of debatable value; Espejo claimed a rich find in silver, but Diego Pérez de Luxán, the chronicler of the expedition, wrote, "We did not find in any of them a trace of silver, as they were copper mines, and poor." At any rate, the Beltrán-Espejo expedition returned to Mexico. Their report stated that they had visited seventy-four Indian pueblos containing an estimated 250,000 natives (an exaggeration). This report stirred considerable interest in the region called New Mexico because the Indians had not been hostile, there were a quarter of a million souls to be saved, the Indians might be put to work to repay the Spaniards for the gift of Christianity, cotton blankets of value had been secured, and there were rumors of rich silver mines.

This report also was forwarded to the royal court at Madrid, and eventually a decision was reached there: New Mexico was to be colonized. However, the receiver of the grant, in return for being named governor and captain-general of the region, had to colonize it at personal expense. Despite the expenditures this would require, many wealthy men vied for the contract. Finally, in 1595, the contract went to Juan de Oñate, heir to a fortune in silver. Oñate set out to fulfill his agreement on February 7, 1598, when he departed northward with four hundred colonists, eighty-three cartloads of baggage, and seven thousand animals, along with a group of Franciscan missionaries. Near present Santa Fe on April 30, 1598, Oñate took formal possession of the province, and the business of colonizing began. The Indians submitted peacefully, and missionaries were sent to their pueblos. By October the little colony seemed to be making sufficiently satisfactory progress for Oñate to go exploring—in search of the Seven Cities and Gran Quivira.

In early October of 1598 he led a small party east but changed his mind upon seeing the High Plains and determined to view the Pacific. Westward he went, reaching the Zuñi pueblo of Hawikúh in November. Hearing rumors of mines to the west, he sent Captain Marcos Farfán to explore. Farfán reached the vicinity of the present Prescott and staked out some mines before returning. At this point Oñate's explorations were interrupted by news of a rebellion at the pueblo of Ácoma. This he suppressed in early 1599 in a bloody siege, after which the remaining Indians were enslaved. Other explorations followed, some led by Oñate and others by his captains. Vicente de Zaldívar, Oñate's nephew, traveled to north-central Arizona in the summer of 1599 but turned back when the horses became jaded and rumors of Indian attack were rife. Oñate led a party to Coronado's Gran Quivira in central Kansas in 1601 but found only disappointment. Finally in October of 1604, with thirty soldiers and two padres, Oñate traveled westward across Arizona to the Colorado River, turned down it, and actually arrived at the mouth of the Colorado River. Rumors of gold and stories of pearls were all he discovered, not the items themselves. This trip ended on April 25, 1605. Again the geography and the native races of Arizona had been described by Spanish explorers, but as yet nothing had been found that would attract permanent settlers.

Oñate was removed as governor and captain-general of New Mexico in 1608 and later was brought to trial on charges of cruelty to the Indians and having found riches which he concealed for his own use. He was convicted on twelve counts in 1614, stripped of his title as governor of New Mexico, exiled permanently from the province and from Mexico City for four years, and heavily fined. Later he was pardoned by the king of Spain in the light of his enormous expenditures incurred in exploring and settling New Mexico.

Oñate's small colony gradually expanded after his departure, as missionaries were sent to more and more outlying pueblos and civilians began farming the fertile valleys. The missionaries reached into Arizona by 1629, working at the Hopi pueblos. Francisco Porrás, Andres

Gutiérrez, and Cristóbal de la Concepción were assigned to the area, called Tusayán, and named their mission San Bernardino. Fray Porrás was poisoned by medicine men jealous of his success in making converts in 1633, but his death did not deter his companions. The Hopis apparently were happy with the missionaries, as shown by their refusal to join Taos Pueblo in a planned revolt against the Spaniards. The padres taught the Hopis to read and write Spanish and instructed them in agricultural methods. When Hopi crops failed in 1659, food was sent to them from Santa Fe to prevent deaths by starvation.

Gradually, however, there was a growing unhappiness among the older Hopis. They saw their traditional way of life—their old religion, ceremonies, and beliefs—being changed. Thus in 1680, when the great New Mexican pueblo revolt broke out, the Hopis joined enthusiastically, killing the four missionaries then in their midst. All Spaniards were driven from New Mexico, leading to the founding of El Paso del Norte (present Juárez, Mexico). The reconquest of the lost province was slow. Not until 1693 was Colonel Diego de Vargas able to pacify the region and visit the Hopi country. Vargas made peaceful overtures, stating there would be no reprisals if the Hopis would swear allegiance to the king of Spain. This the Hopis did, and Vargas left without a fight. But the Hopis never again allowed the Spaniards to occupy their land. They kept their defenses in such a state that only a strong Spanish force could have reduced them. Thus they maintained their independence until the arrival of the Americans 150 years later. These events had significance for Arizona's development, for they meant that Arizona would be colonized from the south, not the east; that Arizona would develop as part of the province of Sonora, not New Mexico; and that Arizona's missions would be established by members of the Society of Jesus (commonly called Jesuits), not by the Franciscans.

To the Ends of the Earth

"In San Cayetano they had prepared us three arbors, one in which to say mass, another in which to sleep, and the third for a kitchen," later wrote Father Eusebio Francisco Kino about his first visit to an Indian village in southern Arizona. This visit, in 1691, marked the entrance of the remarkable Jesuit padre Kino into Arizona and the founding of his mission of San Cayetano de Tumacácori. Gradually he would work northward and westward, mapping, exploring, preaching, and giving agricultural instruction, so that when he died he had added a new region to the Spanish domain.

Born in August, 1645, in the mountainous region between Austria and Italy, Kino was well educated. Early in life he distinguished himself in mathematics and attracted favorable comment from scholars and nobles. By the age of eighteen, he had been offered a professorship at the University of Ingolstadt, but was prevented from taking it by illness so severe that his life was in question. During this illness, he prayed to St. Francis Xavier to intercede for him, promising to enter the Society of Jesus if spared. When he recovered, he kept his promise, even adopting Francisco as a middle name in gratitude. After completing his seminary studies in Bavaria, he asked to be sent to the Orient as a missionary, but he was assigned to New Spain instead. He arrived in Mexico in 1681, and soon was assigned to an attempted colonization of Baja California. There he served as superior of the mission, royal astronomer, surveyor, and map maker. Despite

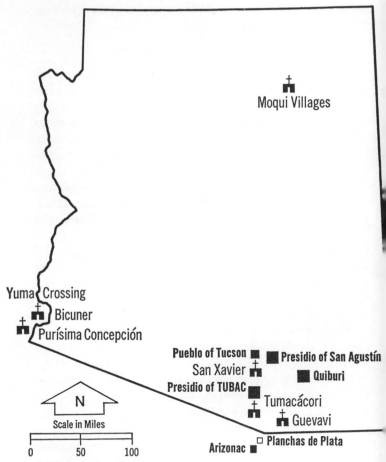

Presidios and missions of Spanish Arizona. *Drawn by Don Bufkin*

hard work, however, the attempt failed, and Kino was reassigned to the present northern Sonora, an area then called *Pimeria Alta* (upper land of the Pima Indians).

In 1687, Kino arrived in Pimería Alta where he founded mission Nuestra Señora de los Dolores. The name was soon shortened to Dolores, and from there he worked north and west, reaching into present Arizona four years later. He extended his activities as far north as the Gila River, establishing not only Tumacácori but also Guevavi and San Xavier del Bac. He was not responsible for the impressive buildings that survive today at Tumacácori and San Xavier del Bac. His establishments were known as *visitas* (temporary structures where he visited to say mass and to baptize). In other parts of Arizona he did not build missions, but he did make itinerant trips to preach and teach.

At these missions and on his trips, Kino taught more than religion. He also was an instructor in agricultural methods. From his established base in the south, he brought horses, mules, sheep, and cattle into Arizona. Within fifteen years after his arrival, he had established the beginnings of ranching in the valleys of the Santa Cruz and the San Pedro in Arizona. He taught the Indians how to care for the animals so that the herds would increase and to butcher and prepare meat for eating. He also introduced various grains and fruits and taught the Indians to plant, harvest, store, and cook these products. Kino always believed that it was easier to teach a well-fed Indian about Christianity than a hungry one, and he took practical steps to insure that the Pimas and Papagos of Arizona were better fed.

Hand in hand with his work as missionary went his activities as explorer and map maker. At least fourteen times he penetrated modern Arizona beyond the line of his missions, making at least six trips to the Gila River and two epic journeys as far west as the Colorado. Since the days of the early conquistadors, Baja California had been regarded as an island; so it was shown in the geography books, and so Kino had been taught in Europe. However, in 1699 he found abalone shells among the Indians along the Gila River, shells which he previously had seen only among the natives of Baja California. Convinced that there must be a land link between the two regions, he made two trips west, finally reaching the mouth of the Colorado in 1702 to write triumphantly, *"California no es isla sino peninsla"* (California is not an island but a peninsula). More often than not Kino made such trips with no military escort, even on occasion with only Indian companions. After such journeys, he called upon his talents as cartographer to produce maps of the region which were widely printed in Europe—and then copied without giving him credit. His definitive map of 1710, showing that Baja California was a peninsula and showing the tribes and geography of Pimería Alta, became the model for all maps of the area for a century.

Constantly he was plagued by shortages of funds. As church and state were one in the Spanish kingdom, he depended upon the royal treasury for his salary (which he used for religious work) and for the money to extend the mission field. The government only grudgingly doled out funds for this work, however, for it too was constantly short, and Kino had to rely on private donations for much of his support. This meant that he had to write lengthy letters to wealthy patrons in Mexico City and the Old World, describing conditions, his work, and his opportunities, to persuade them to contribute.

Despite such labors, he was primarily concerned with the Indians. His multiple trips into Arizona show his love for the natives—he rode or walked an estimated seventy-five thousand miles in the state to reach the Indians. In 1700, at age fifty-five, he averaged forty miles a day for twenty-six straight days. Again, on May 3 that year, he was at Tumacácori mission saying mass at sunrise when a messenger arrived to inform him that at San Ignacio in Sonora an Indian had been sentenced to death by flogging for a minor crime. By nightfall he had ridden sixty-two miles cross-country, not following the roads because they were not straight enough. Early the next morning he rode the last eight miles. In his diary he commented, "I arrived in time to say mass at San Ignacio, and we succeeded in rescuing the prisoner from death." Such feats endeared him to the Indians, who knew he held their best interests at heart.

In 1711, after twenty-four years of labor in Pimería Alta, Kino died at Magdalena, Sonora. A fellow padre described him as a man of courage and frugality: "He prayed much, and was considered without vice. He neither smoked nor took snuff, nor wine, nor slept in a bed. He was so austere that he never took wine except to celebrate mass, nor had any other bed than the sweat blankets of his horse for a mattress and two Indian blankets. He never had more than two coarse shirts, because he gave everything as alms to the Indians."

For the next two decades, Kino's successors proved unworthy followers of their heroic predecessor. Occasionally a padre from the missions of Sonora would ride north to visit the missions of Arizona, but not until 1732 were these permanently staffed. That year Fathers Philipp Segesser and San Juan Bautista Grashoffer arrived to work at San

Xavier del Bac and Guevavi. They were replaced soon afterward by Fathers Ignacio Javier Keller and Jacobo Sedelmayr. Like Kino these two men tried to expand the mission field north. With royal permission to attempt the reconversion of the Hopis, Keller in 1743 made an attempt to preach north of the Gila but was turned back by the Apaches. The next year Father Sedelmayr reached the Casa Grande ruins but could not secure guides willing to brave Apache wrath. Sedelmayr reported that the Apaches interpreted the Spanish desire for peace as a sign of weakness and therefore did not hesitate to attack the newcomers and their converts. There was no military deterrent to such attacks, for the nearest presidio (fort) was at Fronteras, far to the south.

Rumors persisted that the Jesuits had found mines to the north, mines of incredible richness. Such rumors had their origins in the lingering tales of the Seven Cities and the Gran Quivira, which had lured so many Spaniards to the north country. No facts ever supported such charges against the Jesuits, but the stories persisted. Then in 1736 a silver strike was made in southern Arizona, but not by the Jesuits. A Yaqui Indian brought ore samples to a Sonoran merchant, who in turn revealed the find to others, and soon the news became public. It was located at an arroyo known by the Indians as *Arizonac* (probably astride the present international boundary just west of Nogales). Spaniards in incredible numbers rushed to the area, infected by the desire to get rich quick. Estimates of their number vary from five to ten thousand. And some of them did make incredible finds. The silver strangely was in sheets atop the hills and gulleys, and thus the strike became known as the *planchas de plata* (sheets of silver). These "nuggets" averaged from 25 to 50 pounds; one weighed an astounding 425 pounds and was so solid that it resisted attempts to break it into smaller pieces for easy transport. Knowledgeable observers estimated that approximately 10,000 pounds of silver were taken from the area within a few months.

Upon hearing of the strike, the commander of the nearest presidio, Captain Juan Bautista de Anza (the elder) of Fronteras, moved to the area with soldiers to collect the royal taxes. According to Spanish law, all sub-surface deposits were the property of the king, and a tax of 20 per cent was levied on mineral deposits. However, Anza's task was complicated by the nature of the find. The ore was almost pure silver, and, strangely, it was flexible when taken from the ground, resembling a mass of soft wax; but on the following day, after exposure to air, it became hard and inflexible. Anza had to decide if the silver that had been found constituted "ore," on which there was a tax of 20 per cent, or "treasure," on which there was a tax of 95 per cent. Anza collected depositions and sent them to Mexico City for the viceroy's decision, meanwhile impounding all the silver he could find. Eventually the matter was decided in Madrid. The king ruled that the find was a "curiosity," therefore constituting a treasure with the higher tax applying.

Even before this decision could be communicated to Anza, the area had been abandoned. The large—and small—nuggets atop the ground were gone. To tunnel in search of more would have required huge investments, for men and supplies would have had to be brought far north of the line of settlement. Prices for freighting were excessive, and any profits derived would likely have gone to merchants and teamsters rather than to mine operators. And there was the Apache menace. The *Real de Arizonac* (as it was called after the king's decision) lay astride an Apache war trail south, and the miners would have had to fight constantly to hold their claims.

The *Real de Arizonac* did have one lasting effect, however. In 1754 the story was told in an anonymous book published in Barcelona, Spain, entitled *Apostolic Labors of the Company of Jesus*. In 1850 José Francisco Velasco retold the story in his *Noticias Estadísticas del Estado de Sonora* (Statistical Notices of the State of Sonora). Many of the early speculators in Arizona mining were inspired by Velasco's book with its tale of sheets of silver to be found lying on the ground. One early promoter translated the story and used it to sell shares in his mining venture, popularizing the name Arizona to the extent that the territory thereby derived its name. Another effect of Velasco's book was to perpetuate the legend of Jesuit mines, for he cited the earlier work from which he drew the story. Today the legend of the Lost Jesuit Mine (or the Lost Padre's Mine) still lingers, along with numerous other famous "lost" mines and buried treasures, most of which exist only in the imagination.

After the excitement occasioned by the *Real de Arizonac* died away, the region reverted to its quiet status as a missionary outpost. Fathers Keller and Sedelmayr continued their endeavors, searching for heavenly, rather than earthly, riches. By mid-eighteenth century there were eight religious establishments in Pimería Alta with resident missionaries. Keller and Sedelmayr were talking of establishing missions in the Hopi country to the north and near the Colorado River to the west. Beneath the surface of this seeming success with the Indians, however, there were the smouldering hatreds and personal jealousies which brought disaster in 1751.

CROSS AND SWORD IN PIMERÍA ALTA

Late on Saturday evening, November 20, 1751, Father
Jacobo Sedelmayr was informed by a faithful mission Indian, Ignacio Motovit, that the Pimas were planning to
massacre all Spaniards within their region. Sedelmayr
quickly gathered the fourteen Spaniards and Christian
Indians within the vicinity of his mission at Tubutama,
Sonora, along with two soldiers, and they barricaded
themselves inside the religious establishment. Early the
next morning the Sabbath stillness was broken by the
piercing war-cries of some one thousand Pimas gathered
in full war regalia. The natives set fire to the church, but
Sedelmayr and his companions managed to put out the
flames and to hold off the Indians with their firearms. That
night two runners set out for help. Monday passed with
even more furious fighting, but still the defenders held
out with only one of their number being killed. That
night they managed to slip out and, after walking for two
days, reach the safety of the village of Santa Ana, Sonora.
There they learned the full extent of the Pima uprising.

Led by Luís Oacpicagua, who had been recognized as
leading chief of the Pimas by Governor Diego Ortíz de
Parrilla of Sonora, the Pimas planned to kill or drive out
of their land all missionaries, soldiers, ranchers, and Indian sympathizers. Luís had real hopes of success, for in all
of Pimería Alta there were only a few hundred persons
loyal to Spain. And the Pimas were relatively successful.
They killed more than one hundred persons and destroyed
much property; then they retired toward the Santa Catalina Mountains (just north of present Tucson). Few padres
escaped the Pima wrath: Father Tomás Tello was murdered, along with eleven other persons, at Caborca; while

27

at Sonoita Father Enrique Rhuen and two others were killed and the church stripped of its ornaments and burned. Father Francisco Paver, the resident padre at San Xavier del Bac, managed to slip away with three soldiers to Guevavi; with those at that mission, they fled southward to the presidio at Terrenate.

When news of this uprising reached Mexico City, the viceroy immediately ordered measures taken to repair the damage that had been done and to prevent such uprisings in the future. Governor Parrilla led an army to northern Sonora, then sent Captain José Díaz del Carpio to pursue Luís and the fleeing Pimas. Carpio moved to a point some three miles north of Tumacácori mission and established his headquarters at the Indian village of Tubac, arriving there on March 7, 1752. Luís, meanwhile, had taken refuge in the Santa Catalina Mountains and would be difficult to dislodge. Carpio sent scouts into these mountains with word that those Pimas who returned to their pueblos peacefully and who swore allegiance to Spain again would not be harmed. The alternative was war. On March 18, Luís came to Tubac and announced his readiness to accept the terms. Peace had been restored.

Next came the question of blame for the uprising. In the investigation that followed, Governor Parrilla blamed the Jesuits for causing the outbreak, charging them with cruel treatment of the natives. The Jesuits returned the charge, claiming that it was Parrilla who had named Luís captain-general of the Pimas, thus turning his head to thoughts of total rule of Pimería Alta. The Jesuits further charged that immediately after the revolt started, Parrilla committed military blunders which prolonged the war. The quarrel between Parrilla and the Jesuits lasted for years. The investigating committee ruled that there were three main causes of the rebellion: the Indians were unhappy because some of their best lands had been taken by Spaniards; they were angry at punishments meted out by the missionaries to wayward Indians; and Luís had been offended by the padres' refusal to recognize his total headship of the Pimas. Some missionaries were removed, and Governor Parrilla was stripped of his title and transferred.

To prevent another such uprising, the viceroy, the Conde de Revilla Gigedo, ordered that two presidios be constructed, one at Altar and one in the far north. He reported to the king that such a presidio in the far north would "facilitate Spanish advance to the Gila and Colorado rivers." Fifty troops under the command of Captain Tomás de Beldarráin, armed with four small cannon, fifty muskets, and lances, arrived at the Indian village of Tubac and decided to locate the presidio there. San Ignacio de Tubac was situated on the west bank of the Santa Cruz River and thus had an adequate supply of water, even for agriculture. Land suitable for farming was plentiful in the vicinity. It was in the heart of the Pima country where any new revolt could be quickly detected and suppressed. Situated near all three mission establishments in Arizona, this presidio was also on the edge of the Apache raiding trails and might prevent Apache depredations. Under Beldarráin's direction, construction moved rapidly. A walled fort was constructed of adobe. By 1757 the presidio and the small town growing in its shadow contained 411 persons.

In addition to causing the establishment of a permanent Spanish colony in Arizona, the Pima revolt of 1751 had additional effects. Never again would the Jesuits exert real control over the Indians. A few natives did return to their three missions, but mainly those who stopped there did so for convenience. Women and children were left at the missions while the men hunted or made war. The missions also were places of safety during Apache raids. The aged and the ill could be left there and receive free care. The Pimas were no longer rebellious, but mission activity was at a standstill. Also, their revolt stopped the northward movement toward the Gila and Colorado rivers.

Captain Beldarráin died in 1759 and was replaced by a remarkable and tireless soldier, Captain Juan Bautista de Anza. Born at the presidio of Fronteras in 1735, Anza was the son and grandson of presidial commanders. His father had been the captain who tried to collect the king's taxes at the *Real de Arizonac*, and his grandfather had commanded the presidio at Janos for thirty years. Anza grew up on the frontier and was knowledgeable about Indians and their ways. Entering the army at the age of eighteen, he rose rapidly and was commissioned a captain by the time he assumed command at Tubac early in 1760. He proved active and energetic—but fair. Even the missionaries, who normally had few kind words to say about military men, spoke well of him; Father Pedro Font characterized him as "an able and courageous officer." In Arizona he continued to be widely known as a campaigner, one who took battle to the Indians. By 1770, when he petitioned for promotion, he could list two wounds received in the line of duty, recount fourteen general campaigns and many lesser ones in which he had participated, and point out that troops under his command had killed 115 of the enemy, had captured 109 of them, and had recovered more than 2,500 cattle stolen by Indians.

Despite Anza's activities, conditions in Arizona did not significantly improve. With only fifty troops at his presidio, the captain could not make the region secure. Then in the mid-1760's occurred two events that would change the course of Arizona history. First, the end of the Seven Years' War in Europe saw the Louisiana Territory transferred to Spanish control. This removed the French menace to the Spanish colonies and initiated a wave of economizing to recoup the funds spent during the conflict. Second, in 1767 all Jesuits were expelled from the Spanish empire. It was this second event, the expulsion of the Jesuits, that had the most immediate consequences for Arizona.

The causes of the royal order expelling the Jesuits were varied. Some New World officials had complained of growing Jesuit influence. Others declared that the members of this order were too outspoken in their criticism of the royal government. There also were rumors that the Jesuits had found wealthy mines and had not reported them, keeping all the treasure for themselves. Whatever the reasons, the royal decree arrived in Mexico City and had to be followed. Keeping the contents secret, the viceroy sent orders to each presidial commander calling for concerted action. On the same day in June, 1767, all Jesuit priests were taken into custody, quickly and quietly sent to Mexico City, thence to Vera Cruz, and put aboard ships for Europe. All their property, including the missions, was seized by the government. The missions in southern Sonora were secularized (i.e., the buildings became parish churches, while the land and animals were divided among the converts so that they became individual landholders). The religious establishments in Pimería Alta were entrusted to the Franciscan order.

In the interim between the Jesuit expulsion and the arrival of the Franciscans—almost a year—royal *comisa-*

rios were entrusted with the missions and the mission property. When the Franciscans finally arrived in Pimería Alta, they found conditions sadly deteriorated. One wrote, "Some of the establishments had been plundered by the Apaches. . . . In some cases the *comisarios* had grossly neglected their duties." But the real trouble, as the Franciscans saw it, was the Indian converts: "Everywhere the neophytes had been for a year free from all control and had not been improved by their freedom. Not only had they relapsed to a great extent into their roving and improvident habits, but they had imbibed ideas of independence, fostered largely by settlers and soldiers. They regarded themselves as entirely free from all control by the missionaries." In fact, the officers entrusted with the expulsion of the Jesuits had tried to make the Indians regard the change as a release from mission discipline so that they would not become upset by the removal of the Jesuits. When the Franciscans arrived, therefore, they were informed by the Indians that missionaries no longer could give orders but must make requests of native chieftains. If work had to be done, the Franciscans must pay for it. Fortunately for Arizona, the Franciscan sent to San Xavier del Bac proved equal to the challenge.

THE DEVIL'S HIGHWAY

Father Francisco Tomás Garcés arrived at Mission San Xavier del Bac on June 30, 1768. Quickly taking charge there, he soon proved himself a worthy successor to the Jesuits; in fact, he would rival Eusebio Francisco Kino as the most influential missionary ever to work in Arizona during the Spanish period. Rapidly he became the idol of the Pima Indians, who affectionately called him "Old Man," although he was still short of his thirtieth birthday.

A fellow worker characterized him as "so well fitted to get along with the Indians and go among them that he appears to be but an Indian himself. . . . He sits with them in the circle, or at night around the fire, with his legs crossed, and there he will sit musing two or three hours or more, oblivious to everything, talking with much serenity and deliberation. And although the foods of the Indians are as nasty and dirty as those outlandish people themselves, the father eats them with great gusto, and says they are good for the stomach, and very fine." The companion summarized Garcés as missionary by stating, "In short, God has created him, as I see it, solely for the purpose of seeking out these, unhappy, ignorant, and rustic people."

Garcés also carried forward the exploration of the region. Twice he visited the Pimas on the Gila River, and on a third trip he went along Kino's old trail to the junction of the Gila and Colorado rivers. Crossing the Colorado near its mouth, he went west to the terminus of the Cocopah Range at Signal Mountain (near present Calexico). There he met natives who spoke of Europeans to the west who showed some knowledge of the compass and the burning glass. Looking to the northwest from that point, Garcés saw two gaps in the mountains and concluded that an overland route to California existed. Retracing his route to Mission San Xavier, the Franciscan discussed his trip and his conclusions with Captain Juan Bautista de Anza of Tubac presidio. Both were adventurous enough to wish to make an attempt to prove Garcés' conclusion correct. Therefore they sent a formal request to the viceroy to be allowed to undertake the trek.

Viceroy Antonio María Bucareli y Ursua was delighted with the request. California had been colonized in 1769 because the Russians, who were trading and trapping for

furs in Alaska, reportedly were considering the establishment of a colony in California. Under the direction of
José de Gálvez, a brilliant but slightly erratic inspector
general then in New Spain, the colonization project was
undertaken by Captain Gaspar de Portolá and Father
Junípero Serra in 1769–70. San Diego and Monterey were
established, along with five missions, by 1773. However,
the colony's existence was tenuous. Missionaries and soldiers quarreled constantly about lines of authority and
about the soldiers' conduct, which hampered missionary
activity. The most pressing problem was that of supply.
California was linked with New Spain only by shipping,
and the winds along the coast made the voyage unreliable
as a source of steady supply. By 1773 the province contained only sixty-one soldiers and a few Franciscan missionaries. Fortunately the natives had not proved extremely
dangerous. What was desperately needed was an overland
route so that colonists, cattle, horses, and agricultural
implements could be taken to the new province. Thus
Viceroy Bucareli gladly approved the Anza-Garcés request.

Leaving Tubac on January 8, 1773, Anza, Garcés, Father
Juan Díaz, and thirty-four soldiers angled to the southwest
(to a point almost along the present international boundary between Arizona and Sonora). Despite the fact that
they were marching during the period when rain and
snow should have filled all the water holes along their
route, they found the land so dry that the party had to
divide into two parts. The route proved so difficult that
Anza labeled it *el Camino del Diablo* (the Devil's Highway). The two groups reunited near the junction of the
Gila and Colorado rivers, the most critical point on their
trail to California. The Colorado was subject to annual
floods that made it impossible to cross without the co-

operation of the local Indians, the Yumas. The chieftain of this tribe, called Salvador Palma by the Spaniards, was invited to the travelers' camp where he was given a medal in token of his obedience to the Spanish crown. Next Anza's troops demonstrated their firearms by firing at targets, and finally Father Garcés delivered a sermon on the brotherhood of Spaniard and Indian. Palma replied by declaring Yuma friendship with Spain, and the next day he and his tribesmen aided the travelers in crossing the river.

Beyond the Colorado, the Spaniards suffered in the sand dunes for want of water, but managed to reach Mission San Gabriel (present Los Angeles) in California. On the return trip, which proved uneventful, Garcés left the main group and attempted to reach the Hopi Indians of northeastern Arizona; he was able to visit only the Yavapais of northwestern Arizona before turning back. He arrived at Mission San Xavier on July 10, 1774, to discover that Captain Anza had successfully returned and had gone to Mexico City to report personally to Viceroy Bucareli about the overland route to California.

Bucareli was enthusiastic. Immediately he promoted Anza to lieutenant colonel and ordered him to take settlers and supplies over the new route to the struggling province of California. By the end of September, 1775, Anza had recruited 177 colonists in the province of Sinaloa, along with horses, mules, and cattle. Arriving at Tubac, Arizona, the expedition was joined by another 63 persons, bringing the total to 240 people, and stock increases brought that total to 695 horses and mules and 355 cattle. Fathers Garcés, Tomás Eixarch, and Pedro Font also accompanied the expedition. Departing Tubac on October 21, Anza led his expedition north along the Santa Cruz River to the

Gila and down it to the Colorado. He preferred this route, even with the various Indian tribes along the way, to the rigors of the Devil's Highway. Unexpected events did mark this part of the journey. At the first night's camp north of Tubac, one woman gave birth, Anza acting as midwife. Despite his efforts, the mother died. Two other babies were born during the trek, Anza delivering both, and all three infants survived to become Californians.

At the junction of the Gila and Colorado rivers, Chief Salvador Palma came out to greet the expedition—even insisting on embracing every member and expressing his disappointment that they were not coming to colonize at Yuma Crossing. Next he inquired about the health of the viceroy and the king, and was delighted to receive Bucareli's gift: shirt and trousers, jacket with yellow front, blue cape with gold braid, and black velvet cap. At the Yuma village the Spaniards were given watermelons, preserved since harvest by burial in the sand. Once across the Colorado, Father Garcés insisted on remaining to preach the gospel to the Yumas. A small mission was constructed for him on the California side of the river. The rude structure was named Puerto de la Concepción. From the Colorado, Anza led the expedition west in three groups. They suffered from snow and wintry cold, but arrived safely at Mission San Gabriel. A well-traveled road allowed easy passage north to Monterey, where the colonists were placed in another officer's charge. In April, 1776, they became the founders of San Francisco.

On his return trip, Anza found Father Garcés gone from Yuma Crossing on an exploratory trek. While there, he agreed to take Chief Palma to Mexico City to meet the viceroy. At that meeting Palma was dressed in the suit sent to him by Bucareli. On November 11, 1776, Palma signed a document asking baptism for himself and missions for the Yuma Indians. Anza was rewarded by being named governor of New Mexico, while Palma, after a visit in the capital, was returned to his people.

Meanwhile, Father Garcés had been exploring in Arizona and California with an extraordinary idea in mind. Shortly after he had been left at the rude mission constructed for him at Yuma Crossing, he had decided to try opening still another road to California, this one from Santa Fe, New Mexico. On February 14, 1776, he wrote in his diary: "I departed from Puerto de la Concepción in company with two interpreters." These two Yuma Indians guided him up the Colorado for fifteen days (to the vicinity of present Needles, California) where he met Mohave Indians. The Mohaves agreed to furnish him guides for a westward trek. They traveled across the rigorous Mojave Desert, reaching the San Bernardino Mountains. On March 22, Garcés saw the Pacific Ocean in the distance, and soon afterwards he was at Mission San Gabriel. There he rested for two weeks. Then he started back, seeking a new route.

Traveling east toward the Colorado once again, he swung north of his first route into the San Joaquin Valley and the site of the present Bakersfield. On May 30, he was again at the Colorado. Crossing it, he skirted the south rim of the Grand Canyon and, in company with Hualpai Indians, came to the Hopi country of northeastern Arizona. The Hopis proved unfriendly, however, and Garcés could go no farther. On July 3, 1776, he wrote a letter from Oraibe Pueblo in the Hopi country to the Franciscans of New Mexico telling of his journey and recommending that a road be opened from New Mexico westward to California. He then retraced his steps to the Colorado, turned south to Yuma Crossing, and returned to San Xavier mission, arriving on September 17. He had been on the trail for eleven months and had traveled more than two thousand miles. His letter did have the effect of causing an attempt to be made to open a road from New Mexico to California. In the fall of 1776, Fathers Silvestre Escalante and Atanasio Dominguez left New Mexico traveling westward, but they were pushed northward by geography and unfriendly Indians and ended up at the Great Salt Lake instead of California. There their provisions ran short. They decided to return to Santa Fe—and Garcés' hope of a road between the two provinces died.

The Anza-Garcés road to California remained open, however, and colonists and supplies were sent over it regularly to aid the Californians. Viceroy Bucareli realized the usefulness of the route, and he planned settlements at critical points along the way—such as at Yuma Crossing. Radical changes in the administration of the northern provinces (discussed in the next chapter) slowed Bucareli's plans, and thus it was not until February of 1779 that royal permission was given for settlement at the strategic Yuma Crossing. Because of the need for economy, the settlement approved was to be of an experimental nature. Two colonies were to be established there in close proximity, each to consist of two padres, twenty married soldiers, and their families. The two settlements thus would be part presidio, part mission, and part civil settlement. Further economies were effected in the matter of Indian presents; few were sent.

Father Garcés was assigned to this new effort, which became reality in 1780. Both settlements were on the California side of the river, and a similar pattern was followed at both. Town lots and fields were assigned the soldiers, who were allowed to farm in their spare time. The missionaries ministered to civilians, soldiers, and natives alike, for the Indians were not required to live in the mission as was usual at other religious establishments on the frontier. But it was quickly apparent that the Yuma desire for missions had waned, and the miserly allotment of presents greatly disappointed the Indians. Further, they were angered that the Spaniards took some of their best lands for farming. When food supplies ran short during the winter of 1780–81, the Yumas became even more disenchanted with the Spanish newcomers, for both were competing for the mesquite beans that all were eating.

The Yuma discontent came to a head in the summer of 1781. In June, Captain Fernando de Rivera y Moncada, the lieutenant governor of California, arrived from Sonora with a group of colonists bound westward. The captain proved a strict disciplinarian of Indians, but he did not restrain his soldiers or the civilians from taking what they wanted from the Yumas. When the colonists departed for California, Rivera y Moncada and his soldiers lingered on the east bank of the river. The Yumas determined on revenge and plotted in secret. On July 17 they struck with sudden swiftness at the two settlements on the west bank, killing the men and enslaving the women and children. Garcés and another padre were spared for two days, but martyred on July 19. On the morning of July 18, the Yumas struck the unsuspecting Spanish soldiers on the east bank of the river and clubbed them to death. Garcés died at age forty-three, his road with him. Governor Felipe de Neve of Sonora made no effort to avenge the Yuma uprising. The culprits for this uprising, he told higher authorities, were Anza and Garcés; they had misrepresented the Yumas as peaceful. Colonel Pedro Fages arrived in September to ransom the captive women and children and to gather the bones of the martyred padres for reburial elsewhere, but he made no attempt to fight the Indians. Yuma hostility prevented further immigration to California by the overland highway, and Arizona's connection with the neighboring province was ended for half a century.

LANCERS FOR THE KING

"It seems that the number and boldness of the hostile Indians increases every day," declared Charles III, king of Spain, in 1772. He therefore decreed that drastic changes be made in the administration of the northern provinces of New Spain, along with new methods of garrisoning the presidios and of supplying them. This decree, known as the Royal Regulations of 1772, came about as a result of the end of the Seven Years' War in Europe. At the termination of that conflict, fought largely for supremacy in North America, England emerged the victor, gaining Canada and Florida. The French, who had been eliminated from the colonial race, ceded the Louisiana Territory west of the Mississippi River to Spain as compensation for its loss of Florida; Louisiana east of the river went to England. No longer were Spaniards faced with French enemies on the northeastern frontier; the frontier had moved east, bringing a new enemy, the English. The expensive military posts in East Texas could be abandoned, a boon to the depleted Spanish treasury. In fact, such changes caused the Spanish monarch to decide to completely overhaul the colonial policy along the northern frontier. To accomplish this purpose, the Marqués de Rubí was commissioned in 1766 to make a tour of inspection from the Gulf of California to the Gulf of Mexico with an eye to accomplishing economies while at the same time reducing the number of Indian raids.

Between 1766 and 1768 the marqués made his tour, accompanied by a talented military engineer, Nicolás de Lafora. Tubac, the only military post in Arizona, did not impress either man. There they reported fifty muskets, fifty lances, fifty swords, and forty leather coats (used as a type of armor to ward off Indian arrows). "There are also . . . four four-pounder cannon cast in Mexico, neither good looking nor well made," wrote Lafora. "Two of these at Tubac are totally useless because fire flashes from cracks in the breech. The majority of the others are rusty, and that [fact], plus the ignorance of the people handling them, has caused many accidents." Rubí's recommendations, presented in Mexico City in 1769, called for the presidio at Tubac to be moved down the Santa Cruz River (to the north) to the site of a Sobaipuri and Pima Indian village called Tucson. To control the Apaches, Rubí recommended a policy of extermination by military means, in line with which the presidios along the northern frontier were to be arranged in a cordon of fifteen posts some 120 miles apart stretching from Sonora to Texas.

Another official, José de Gálvez, likewise was inspecting the northern frontier in the late 1760's. In his capacity as visitador-general, Gálvez was to recommend administrative changes. His report stressed that the northern region, which he called the Interior Provinces, were far removed from Mexico City and the viceroy's close personal attention, yet were the provinces that most needed a strong administrator. Gálvez therefore suggested that the Interior Provinces be separated from the viceroyalty of New Spain and placed under the command of a military officer. This official's headquarters should be in the Interior Provinces so that quick decisions could be reached at times of crisis. In short, he recommended the creation of an office combining civil, military, and judicial functions and answerable to the king, not the viceroy.

In 1772 the king agreed to part of the Gálvez-Rubí recommendations in the Royal Regulations. The Interior Provinces were placed under the supervision of a commandant-inspector, but not separate from the viceroyalty. These regulations also carefully prescribed arms, equipment, mounts, and rations for the soldiers, as well as pay, discipline, and the militia, in an attempt to end abuses that had crept into the presidial system. But the commandant-inspector was to receive his funds from the viceroy, not directly from the royal treasury. Commissioned to this office in 1772 was Colonel Hugo O'Conor, an Irish mercenary in Spanish service. Actively and courageously O'Conor sought to carry out the intent of the Royal Regulations—which was to do by military means what the mission had failed to do through gentle persuasions, subdue the Indian foe. Several campaigns were conducted in Chihuahua, New Mexico, and Sonora. O'Conor also moved the presidio of Tubac north to Tucson late in 1776; across the river from the Indian village, construction began on adobe walls of Presidio San Agustín del Tucson. Despite these moves, however, the frontier provinces of New Spain continued to deteriorate as hostile Indians raided almost at will. Therefore in 1776 the king fully implemented the Gálvez-Rubí recommendations, creating the Interior Provinces separate from the viceroyalty of New Spain and placing them under the command of a commandant-general.

First to occupy this post was Brigadier General Teodoro de Croix, a native of Lille, France, and an able, energetic, and knowledgeable officer. Croix in the late 1770's did carry on campaigns against the Apaches as Rubí had recommended. As commander at Tucson he designated Captain Pedro Allande y Saabedra, a Spaniard of noble birth and twenty-two years of experience in the army. By 1778, Allande y Saabedra had seventy-seven soldiers at his fort. These men not only had to protect settlers in the area and guard the missions, but also to construct the presidio at Tucson. Allande y Saabedra also found time for campaigns into the hostiles' territory in 1778, and he defeated some 350 Apaches who attacked Tucson on November 6, 1779. Owing to Spanish expenses as allies of the United States in its war of revolution, 1779–83, frontier campaigns were curtailed, preventing reprisals against the Yuma Indians when they destroyed the Spanish settlements there and martyred Father Garcés. The Apaches grew bolder during this period of Spanish inactivity, and on May 1, 1782, approximately 300 of them attacked at Tucson. Captain Allande y Saabedra had only 24 soldiers on hand at the time, but again he was able to force the hostiles to retreat.

The year 1783 saw Allande y Saabedra taking the offensive, pushing as far north as the Gila River into Apache territory. Again the following year he went north, this time as far as present Solomonville, and in 1785 he probed the Gila Valley and the Huachuca Mountains to the southeast. Such campaigns did little to settle the Apache problem, however. There were too many Indians and too few Spanish soldiers—and the soldiers were not properly equipped and trained for desert warfare against warriors such as the Apaches. As offensive weapons, these *soldados de cuera*, as they were called, carried a musket, two pistols, a lance, and a short sword. The sword and lance were designed for war against an enemy that stood and fought hand to hand, as was traditional in Europe but useless against the Indians. Their firearms proved almost worthless in Spanish Arizona because of inadequate training in their use and maintenance. Also, Spanish regulations provided that each soldier be issued only three pounds of gunpowder annually. Since a soldier had to purchase all powder used in excess of that three pounds, he had little incentive in target practice.

For defensive purposes, the soldier carried a shield (*adarga*) and wore a leather coat (*cuera*) and leather leggings (*botas*). All were bulky, cumbersome, and hot—and practically useless. Thus armed for offense and defense, the presidial troops constituted heavy cavalry, requiring some six remounts each on expeditions against the Indians. General Croix urged that the shield, the leather jacket, and the lance be discarded. He argued that the use of lightly equipped, mounted troops employing the latest firearms and the best horses might be able to pursue the Indians to their villages and even to defeat them in battle. But Croix's suggestions were not implemented in the Interior Provinces to any great extent; presidial officers preferred the lance and the leather armor since these were both traditional and inexpensive. When General Croix was promoted to the post of viceroy of Peru in 1783, conditions in the Interior Provinces had not markedly improved. Following his departure, command of the Interior Provinces was divided into Eastern and Western Interior Provinces with both divisions again under overall control of the viceroy.

Then in 1786 came a new offensive and defensive policy for the Interior Provinces, a change that would have long-range consequences for Arizona. That year Bernardo de

Gálvez became viceroy of New Spain. A nephew of José de Gálvez, the new viceroy had extensive administrative and frontier experience. From his knowledge of frontier conditions, he formulated his *Instructions for the Governing of the Interior Provinces of New Spain* in 1786. In this plan, Gálvez decreed a vigorous war on those Indians not at peace with Spain. Once the hostiles asked for peace, they were to be settled in villages in the shadow of a presidio, where they would be given presents, inferior firearms, and alcoholic beverages. He reasoned that the presents would be of such value that the Indians would prize peace more than war and that the arms supplied them would quickly become inoperative and could be repaired only by Spaniards. The intent of the *Instructions* was to corrupt the Indian will to resist and make the hostiles dependent on Spaniards. Gálvez made this clear: "After all, the supplying of drink to the Indians will be a means of gaining their goodwill, discovering their secrets, calming them so they will think less often of conceiving and executing their hostilities, and creating for them a new necessity which will oblige them to recognize their dependence upon us more directly."

In connection with the Gálvez policy, Captain Manuel de Echeagaray led a combined expedition, consisting of soldiers drawn from the presidios of Santa Cruz and Altar in Sonora and Tucson in Arizona, and campaigned along the headwaters of the Gila in 1788. That same year Captain Pablo Romero, the acting commandant at Tucson, conducted a month-long campaign that killed forty-four Apaches. Such expeditions had success, for soon the Apaches were begging for peace. They were settled in what were called *establecimientos de paz* (establishments of peace) in Sonora and at Tucson. Captain José de Zúñiga assumed command at Tucson in 1794 and proved most active in pushing the Apaches to accept peace. A native of Sonora, Zúñiga had enlisted as a private at the age of seventeen and had risen to the rank of lieutenant within eight years. Arriving at Tucson in 1794 at the age of thirty-nine, he remained at the Old Pueblo until 1810. Several times he took the field against hostiles, reaching as far north as the Zuñi pueblos in 1795. Conquered Apaches were forced to live at Tucson. There they were given a weekly ration of corn, meat, tobacco, and candy. They were allowed to keep their weapons and their tribal customs—to the disgust of the Franciscan missionaries. The intent was corruption, not Christianization. The Apaches in the *establecimiento de paz* at Tucson, complained Father Diego Bringas de Manzaneda, learned card playing, gambling, dancing, swearing, and drunkenness. In short, he said, they had accepted all the vices of the Spaniards, had added them to their indigenous vices, and had neither retained their own virtues nor adopted any of the Spanish virtues.

Nevertheless, the Gálvez policy did bring a period of peace to Arizona. Ranching, mining, and farming could now proceed with relative safety, while the Franciscans, who complained against the new system, were free to build impressive and beautiful structures at Tumacácori and Tucson. Both locations had been raided repeatedly previous to the 1780's. Once peace had been established, civilians could venture into Arizona. At Tucson and at the old presidial location of Tubac, settlers began to locate. In 1804, Zúñiga reported thirty-seven Spanish civilians along with 200 Indians. Four thousand cattle, 2,600 sheep, and 1,200 horses grazed in the vicinity of Tucson, while cotton, grown by the Indians, was used to make clothing. Some 1,000 cattle were at Tubac in 1804, along with a few settlers. As these figures indicate, ranching was the major occupation in Arizona other than soldiering. From this era dated the large land grants, such as the Canoa and the Sonoita. The largest such operation, however, was not near Tucson or Tubac but at San Bernardino (where John Slaughter later would establish his famous ranch). In 1822 this grant was sold to Ignacio Pérez, an army lieutenant, who at one time reportedly had 100,000 head of cattle on this barony.

Mining activity was minimal during the Spanish period. A lime mine north of Tucson was supplying local needs, while precious metals were being secured near Arivaca and in the Santa Rita Mountains east of Tubac (the Salero Mine). Farming was mainly of a subsistence nature—corn, beans, and chiles—for local consumption. By 1819, as the Spanish era was drawing to a close, Tucson boasted a population of sixty-two in addition to the soldiers and their families, who owned some 5,600 head of cattle and numberless flocks of sheep.

The Mexican War of Independence, which began in 1810 and was crowned with success in 1821, was of no consequence for Arizona. Local soldiers and civilians were not involved. Captain José Romero, who commanded at the end of Spanish control, continued as commander during the early years of Mexican rule. Commandant-General of the Western Interior Provinces in 1821, Antonio Cordero y Bustamante notified Romero of the change and instructed him to assemble his officers and soldiers, along with the civilians, and ask them to take the oath of independence. At this ceremony each officer came before a crucifix and a book of the Gospels which had been placed on a table. They then swore upon the hilts of their swords to be obedient to the Catholic faith, to preserve the independence of Mexico, and to work to achieve peace and harmony between natives and Europeans. Civil and religious officials, along with the people, took the same oath before an upraised crucifix. Thus ended some three centuries of Spanish rule—quietly and with dignity.

SONORA NORTH TO APACHERIA

Tucson—which constituted the only major settlement in Arizona in 1821—was not impressive when the Mexican flag first was raised above it. Built in the form of a square, it was enclosed by 10- to 12-foot-high walls some 750 feet long. These walls were 3 feet thick at the base, constructed of adobe bricks, measuring 4-by-12-by-18 inches, held together by mortar of a dark brown color. The soldiers' quarters were along the south wall, the roof serving as a parapet as did the roofs along the other three sides. Stables ran along the north wall, while civilian homes were adjacent to the east and west walls. Only one gate allowed entry; above it was a station for a sentinel. Other buildings were scattered inside the city, including the church, which measured some 10-by-20 feet. Three plazas gave open space for drilling the troops, dancing, courtship, and other recreational activities: the *Plaza Militar* in front of the stables, the *Plaza de las Armas* before the soldiers' quarters, and the *Plaza Iglesia* before the church. Only one store was inside this enclosure, a saloon dispensing mescal owned by Juan Burruel. Outside the wall were three other stores which sold less necessary items.

Few of the living quarters inside the city had windows. Doors generally were made of brush or cactus ribs tied with rawhide. A small fireplace built in a corner served as cookstove and source of heat. The residents generally slept on the floor rolled in blankets. Chairs and tables were in short supply, as were most types of furniture; therefore meals were served on the floor or on the ground outside the hut. Perhaps a trunk or chest held the family's scant possessions, which seldom included more than a few pieces of clothing, cooking utensils, and religious objects. Cock fights, horse racing, observance of the local patron saint's day, gambling, and *fandangos* (dances) provided relief from the tedium, hard work, and danger which constituted their lives.

Few of these residents were literate enough to care about the political system of the new Republic of Mexico or to inquire about their place in it. Technically the area now known as Arizona became a part of *El Estado Libre de Occidente* (the Free State of the West), which also included the present Mexican states of Sonora and Sinaloa. Created in 1824, Occidente by the following year had a constitution which provided for executive, legislative, and judicial branches of government. Curiously, the legislature was to have only one house. Therein lay the seeds of destruction of the state of Occidente. Of the eleven seats in this body, six were to be filled by residents of the present Sinaloa and five by Sonorans. Sinaloa and Sonora were too different in geography, economy, and problems to continue as one, however. And Sonorans were angry at being dominated by Sinaloans. A separatist movement in Sonora achieved its ends in 1831, after which Arizona became a part of Sonora. Thus it would continue until it became a part of the United States.

The political history of Occidente and Sonora—and thus Arizona—in the years 1821–46 reflected the confusion of the national government during this same period. In this quarter-century there were twenty-three governors, as wily politicians contended to command the destiny of the state. Mainly this struggle was between centralists and federalists, or between those who wished the central government to dominate the country and those who wanted a federal republic with power divided between the national government and the states. In Sonora the two individuals who came to personify the opposing philosophies were José Urrea, the federalist, and Manuel María Gándara, the centralist. Urrea was a native Tucsonan, born there in 1797. A royalist during the Mexican revolution, he later became a republican although he would support the dictatorial ambitions of Antonio López de Santa Anna, the leader responsible for much of the unrest in Mexico until 1855. Gándara, born in 1800 near the town of Pitic, Sonora, was a lawyer of royalist sympathies who believed in a strong central government and became the acknowledged leader of the ultraconservatives in Sonora. The fortunes of these two men waxed and waned according to the political tides in Mexico City, as they succeeded each other by revolution frequently. What each sought was power more than principle.

Arizona was isolated from these power struggles by scant population, poverty, and apathy. Its few residents were more interested in the daily fight for survival than they were in political maneuvers. The constitutions of both Occidente and Sonora provided for limited local self-government. Following Spanish tradition, these allowed small cities to install an *alcalde* of police and a *sindico procurador* (advocate); in actual practice in Arizona, the civil, judicial, and executive authority was exercised by the presidial commander, who acted as a deputy governor for the state. Three men would occupy

A composite likeness of Eusebio Francisco Kino, the Jesuit priest who established permanent missions in Arizona. *Arizona Pioneers' Historical Society*

Tumacacori National Monument. *Arizona Pioneers' Historical Society*

San Xavier del Bac, the "White Dove of the Desert," is often called the most beautiful Spanish mission in North America. *Arizona Pioneers' Historical Society*

A diorama depicting José Romero and Father Felix Caballero leaving Tucson for California in 1823. *Arizona Pio-*

Tucson in 1862. *From J. Ross Brown's* Adventure in the Apache Country.

Sylvester Mowry, one of the "Founding Fathers" of Arizona. *Arizona Pioneers' Historical Society*

Charles D. Poston mined in southern Arizona and lobbied for the creation of the Territory of Arizona. *Arizona Pioneers' Historical Society*

John Robert Baylor, Confederate governor of Arizona. *George W. Baylor, Jr.*

General James H. Carleton, commander of the California Column and self-proclaimed Union governor of Arizona. *Arizona Pioneers' Historical Society*

that post at Tucson during the Mexican era: Captains José Romero, 1821–30, José Antonio Comaduran, 1830–53, and Hilarion García, 1853–56. Romero is best remembered as the "Mexican Anza," a nickname he earned by briefly reopening the Anza-Garcés road to California.

Early in May of 1823, Father Felix Caballero, a Dominican padre laboring in missions in Baja California, arrived in Tucson after traveling overland from his home at San Miguel, Baja California. With permission from the commanding general, Romero and Caballero departed Tucson with ten soldiers on June 8, intending to bypass the hostile Yuma Indians and reach California. They went northward to the Gila River and down it almost to its junction with the Colorado, then angled to the southwest to cross the Colorado near its mouth. The natives in that vicinity seemed friendly and aided the Mexicans across the river, but then they treacherously stole most of their baggage. By mid-July the expedition was at Caballero's mission of San Miguel. From there they traveled the regular road north to San Diego. Romero reported, "The road from Tucson is short. . . . It can be covered in ten or eleven days; but there is the obstacle of the Colorado River." More specifically, he meant the obstacle of the Yuma Indians. The news of this exploit was hailed in newspapers in Mexico City, and soon afterward Romero was promoted to lieutenant colonel, just as Anza had been. Romero began his return trip in November, seeking a route north of Yuma Crossing, but became lost in the Mojave Desert and had to return to the coast. Not until December of 1825 was Romero able to return to Tucson— and the route to California remained closed owing to Indian hostility.

Comaduran had been serving at Tucson since before

independence and thus was knowledgeable and experienced when he was promoted to captain and assumed command of the post in 1830. Born in 1789 in the New World, he had enlisted as a private at the age of seventeen and had risen through the ranks. His was the task of trying to stay Apache hostility with only 50 troops at his command. The Mexican central government, just as the Spanish government which preceded it, never formulated any real strategy for the frontier provinces. In 1826 the secretary of War and Marine, Gomez Pedraza, decreed that the presidio at Tucson "should" have 6 officers and 94 men, and in 1848 Secretary of War and Marine Mariano Arista published a decree stating that the presidio at Tucson "should" have 7 officers and 143 men. In actual practice, the presidio existed during these years with 3 officers and 49 men, woefully inadequate to its tasks. The Indians roamed and raided almost at will.

During the Mexican War of Independence and in the years immediately following, the Apaches, the most warlike tribe in Arizona, remained at peace. As late as 1827 the British ambassador in Mexico, Henry Ward, commented on a visit to Sonora that the Apaches were not troubling the inhabitants. The Indians had fought the Spaniards, he asserted, because the Spaniards had taken the natives' best lands. The Mexicans had more land than they required, however, and Ward saw "little reason to fear an interruption of the good understanding which at present prevails." Four years later, in 1831, the Apaches thundered out of the north, ending the period of peace, apparently in the belief that the Mexican government was not going to continue the distribution of presents which the Spaniards had begun in 1786. The Sonoran response was to return to the policies instigated by the

Royal Regulations of 1772—warfare. They would force the Apaches to the peace table by might of arms. Unfortunately for Sonorans, the central government did not support this effort with the necessary pesos, and the campaign faltered. In October of 1833 the governor of Sonora issued a plea for public donations to finance militia campaigns. The following year the state, in a move of desperation, cut the salary of its public officials from 10 to 33 per cent, the money to be used to raise and equip an army. A small force took the field in the summer of 1834, but the cut in salaries produced more complaints and the fighting men even fewer results. Four months later full salaries were restored to all government officials.

The national government responded to the desperate pleas from Sonora and Chihuahua by reprinting the Royal Regulations of 1772, even to the signature of *"Yo El Rey"* (I the King), in 1834. But what was needed was competent leadership and efficient, well-equipped soldiers, not reprints of a military plan that had failed six decades earlier. When it became evident that no help was forthcoming from the central government and that salary cuts, pleas for donations, and abortive treaties with the Indians had produced no positive results, the situation in Sonora grew desperate. From the mid–1830's until the American conquest of Arizona, the population of Sonora actually declined, although it was increasing in other parts of Mexico. Arizpe, the capital city of the state, had numbered seven thousand residents in 1821 but in 1846 boasted only fifteen hundred, and the capital was removed to Ures as a result of increasing Indian pressures. Tucson and Tubac were besieged on several occasions by as many as one thousand warriors, but these attacks were repulsed because the settlers could take refuge within the walls of the presidios.

53

At the end of the Mexican era, no means of curbing the Apache menace had been found.

Missions, which once had been the Spanish hope for bringing peace to the frontier, were no answer to Arizona's needs during the Mexican period, for they had ceased to exist. Those padres who refused to take the oath of independence had been expelled in 1821. San Xavier del Bac, near Tucson, was without a resident missionary for years as a result, and its buildings were used as stables, barns, and barracks. Tumacácori fared much better for a time. Father Ramón Liberós took charge in 1822, and that year he sold four thousand head of cattle from the mission's holdings. Liberós even continued the unfinished work of construction at Tumacácori. However, Mexican independence had never been recognized by Spain, and war between the two nations seemed imminent. The Mexican Congress on December 20, 1827, decreed that all foreign missionaries be expelled, and Liberós, a Spaniard, was unceremoniously escorted away from Tumacácori by soldiers early in 1828. San Xavier and Tumacácori thereafter were visited only by occasional missionaries who traveled north from Sonora.

Then, on April 16, 1834, the Mexican Congress passed a law secularizing all remaining missions. Until this date San Xavier and Tumacácori technically were church property, although they were in increasingly dilapidated condition. Eight more years passed, years during which the Indians continued to live at Tumacácori. No one wanted the land. Finally, in 1842, the Mexican government decreed that abandoned lands valued at less than $500 could be sold at public auction. On April 19, 1844, the treasury department of the state of Sonora auctioned Tumacácori's land—52,000 acres—to Francisco Aguilar, a brother-in-law of Governor Gándara, who shortly assumed ownership. There Gándara constructed a woolen factory employing eighteen persons; twenty-two shepherds cared for ten thousand sheep and six hundred goats. Gándara abandoned this land in 1855. Thereafter it passed through various owners, finally to become Tumacacori National Monument on September 15, 1908. San Xavier continued to deteriorate until 1913 when it again became Franciscan property (as it is today, still serving the spiritual needs of the Papago Indians).

With no missions in existence after 1828—and only occasional visits by padres—Arizonans could not hope to end the Apache menace through conversion to Christianity. As military coercion by the state had failed and no hope remained of national aid, Sonoran officials in the late 1830's turned to the scalp-bounty system, an ancient Spanish practice. Anyone bringing in an Apache scalp would be paid one hundred pesos (a peso was worth one dollar American) for the scalp of adult males, fifty pesos for the scalp of a squaw, and twenty-five pesos for children's scalps. The law did not work as intended, however, for examining committees could not tell the difference between the hair of hostile savages and that of friendly Indians. Soon almost all natives were on the warpath. Also, examining committees found it difficult to tell the difference between Indian scalps and the hair of Mexicans —with the result that entire Mexican villages were depopulated by greedy, unscrupulous bounty hunters and the hair of the residents turned in to the government for the grisly reward. In 1837, James Johnson demonstrated the profits to be reaped. That year he went to the Apache village of Juan José, where he was known, with sacks of "treats." Inside one sack was a small loaded cannon, its barrel plugged shut. When the Indians crowded around, Johnson touched his cigar to the cannon and walked away. The resulting explosion killed almost all the Indians, and Johnson and his men calmly scalped the dead. One Indian escaped, a relative of Juan José named Mangas Coloradas, later to become a famed and deadly enemy of Americans. The most successful of the bounty hunters was James Kirker, a former trapper and mountain man who, with some two hundred followers, collected fabulous sums for scalps. In 1839, for example, he collected a reported $100,000.

Several Americans other than James Johnson and James Kirker were coming into Arizona during the Mexican years. They too were seeking pelts, but their quarry was beaver, not Indian scalps. These fur trappers were the advance guard of the westward-moving pioneers. They came because beaver in the northern streams were becoming scarce and because New Mexico, along with the rest of Mexico, had been opened to foreigners with the coming of independence from Spain. Taos and Santa Fe became headquarters for this southwestern trapping activity. The Gila River became the path of entry, and from it these men spread to almost every stream in Arizona. Often they were colorful individuals. In the region of the Little Colorado and the San Francisco peaks lived William Sherley "Old Bill" Williams, a skillful and hardy mountain man. Something of a hermit, he liked and usually wore Indian clothing, and he preferred to sleep on the ground, even in the coldest part of winter. His red hair and gaunt, weather-beaten face were well known. After months in the mountains, he would return to Taos with enough pelts to finance several weeks of drinking, gambling, and carousing, after which he would set out again, alone, to seek more pelts. He left his name on a mountain and a river.

Other mountain men in Arizona during the Mexican era included Antoine Leroux, a French trapper who worked in northern Arizona, and Paulino Weaver, a son of Tennessee who left his name carved on the Casa Grande ruins in 1832 before settling in California on a land grant given to him by the Mexican governor. During the American period he settled at Prescott, where he worked as army scout, guide for prospectors, and friend of the Indians. Ewing Young was a lesser-known trapper whose fame rests more on the quality of his followers than on his own deeds, daring though these were. Young organized expeditions that first brought Christopher "Kit" Carson to Arizona and California, as well as James Ohio Pattie. Kit Carson later would win a lasting reputation as an army scout and soldier, while James Ohio Pattie would dictate to Timothy Flint his adventures (*Personal Narrative . . .*), a story of high adventure still widely read.

These mountain men were few in number, their visits to Arizona only occasional, but they portended the future. To the south, where there was political turmoil, only scant attention was paid to frontier regions such as Arizona. During the Mexican period, Sonora (and thus Arizona) was regarded as a kind of "Siberia" or "the end of the world." Immigration to the region doubtless would have occurred if the government had provided protection from Apache incursions. However, this was not done, and the population diminished. Then, in the mid–1840's, growing tensions between the United States and Mexico brought this region into sharp focus, and its ownership became of interest to both nations. At that time the population of Arizona, including Christian Indians, numbered approximately six hundred, and the features of the land were almost unchanged from the way nature first fashioned them, with the Indians enjoying almost total domain.

Part Two: **THE TERRITORIAL YEARS**

Yanquis Southwest

The causes of the Mexican War were far removed from Arizona. The origins of this conflict can be traced to a clash of cultures, to the claims question (the debts owed by Mexico to American citizens but which Mexico consistently refused to pay), to the American desire for California, to the question of the Texas boundary, and to the unwillingness of Mexican politicians to seek a peaceful solution. French military advisers had told Mexican officials that they could win a war with the United States. Therefore these politicians were making irresponsible statements to the effect that they would see "the Eagle and Serpent flying over the White House" before they would negotiate a settlement. President James K. Polk sought every honorable avenue of settlement but still did not go before the Congress to request a declaration of war until Mexican troops attacked American soldiers north of the Río Grande in April of 1846. Congress responded on May 12 with a declaration of war.

Arizona had no major cities, no known mines, and no real strategic value in this conflict. Therefore nothing transpired there that significantly altered the outcome of the war. The columns of Generals Zachary Taylor and Winfield Scott never reached Arizona. In fact, the American soldiers who did enter Arizona did so as transients, not as occupiers. Colonel, later Brigadier General, Stephen Watts Kearny was authorized, just after the outbreak of war, to organize the "Army of the West," which he did at Independence, Missouri. With this army he marched to Santa Fe, where Governor Manuel Armijo surrendered without firing a shot. Kearny thereupon split his army into four parts: the first to remain at Santa Fe as an army of occupation; the second under Colonel Alexander W. Doniphan to march south to Chihuahua City and then east to link up with Taylor; the third, consisting of three hundred dragoons, he personally would lead to California to effect its conquest; and the fourth under Lieutenant Colonel Philip St. George Cooke was to open a wagon road from New Mexico to California.

On September 25, 1846, Kearny led his three hundred men south down the Río Grande, then turned west toward the Gila, intending to follow this river to its junction with the Colorado and thence to California. While still in New Mexico, he met Kit Carson coming east with dispatches stating that California already had been conquered by Americans. Captain John Charles Frémont and Commodore Robert F. Stockton had effected this conquest, and Carson was bearing their letters of this success east. Kearny sent two hundred of his dragoons back to Santa Fe and persuaded Carson to guide him and the remaining one hundred men to California. As they progressed down the Gila River, they met roving bands of Apaches who proved peaceful if not friendly. The Apaches had long hated the Mexicans, and they regarded the Americans, who were at war with Mexico, as allies—even offering to aid in the conquest of Chihuahua if Kearny was inclined to invade that state. In central Arizona, Kearny met the Pima Indians, who proved even friendlier than the Apaches. When Kearny's army needed flour from the Pimas, who raised wheat, the Pimas refused money, saying, "Bread is to eat, not to sell; take what you want." At the junction of the Colorado and Gila rivers, Kearny's dragoons captured four Mexican herders who informed the Americans that a counterrevolution was under way in California. Kearny crossed the Colorado, departing the pages of Arizona history as he headed for defeat at the hands of the insurgents in the Battle of San Pascual on December 6–10 in California.

Meanwhile, Philip St. George Cooke was undertaking his task of opening a wagon road from Santa Fe to San Diego. His five hundred men constituted the famed Mormon Battalion, members of the Church of Jesus Christ of Latter-day Saints whose pay was being used to finance the Mormon move to Utah. On October 21, 1846, the march began at Santa Fe. Cooke followed the Río Grande south, making about ten miles a day, until November 10, when he turned to the west. Across this arid stretch the battalion marched. Some days they found water; other days they did not. Finally they reached Playas Lake (present Hidalgo County, New Mexico), where they drank their fill. Soon thereafter they found the road running from Janos, Chihuahua, to the San Bernardino Ranch in extreme southeastern Arizona. Guided by Antoine Leroux and Paulino Weaver, they arrived at San Bernardino to find it abandoned and the cattle running wild. In fact, the battalion was attacked by wild, ferocious bulls. A private was tossed in the air and gored in the leg. The same bull eviscerated a mule before being felled by rifle fire. Colonel Cooke, when confronted by an enormous bull, prepared to make a run for his life. Luckily, a corporal shot the animal, and it died practically at Cooke's feet. Lieutenant George Stoneman almost shot off his own thumb while trying to kill a bull. Cooke in his journal referred to this incident as "The Battle of Bull Run," anticipating the Civil War battle by some fifteen years.

On December 12 the guide Leroux, who had been scouting, returned with information gained from some Mexicans he had found making mescal; they had informed him that the garrison at the presidio of Tucson had been increased to two hundred men. Cooke had his men load their weapons, and he gave them a briefing on military tactics. Then he advanced toward Tucson. On the morning of December 14 a small party of Mexican soldiers appeared under a flag of truce bearing a message from Captain José Antonio Comaduran, commandant at Tucson. Comaduran's message said that he had orders not to allow the Americans to march through Tucson but that he would not molest them if they marched quietly around the city. Cooke replied that these terms were unacceptable. The next morning still another deputation of Mexicans came out to arrange, as they said, an armistice. Cooke demanded that the garrison surrender, the town be thrown open to trade and refreshment for his men, and token arms forfeited. If these terms were met, he promised to parole the Mexican soldiers. The Mexicans responded that such terms were unacceptable to Comaduran. Thus Cooke and the Mormons approached the Old Pueblo on December 16 expecting a hot fight—but they found Comaduran and the garrison had fled during the night. The city was open to them.

Entering Tucson, Cooke ordered the public stores of food thrown open to his men, many of whom proceeded to eat themselves sick. For two days the Mormon Battalion rested at Tucson. During the night of December 17–18, there was a brief flurry of excitement when a rumor spread that Comaduran had returned to attack. The officer of the day became so excited that he shouted, "Beat that drum, beat that drum—if you can't beat that drum, beat that fife!" Cooke restored order, then sent a detail to reconnoiter the town. Soon he had to send another detail to look for the first one. There was no attack, but the night was lost for sleep.

As the battalion prepared to depart on the morning of December 18, Cooke left a message which possibly was an attempt to stir sedition in Arizona and Sonora. To Governor Gándara he wrote that Sonora had suffered many wrongs at the hands of negligent Mexican politicians and suggested that "the unity of Sonora with the states of the North, now her neighbors, is necessary effectually to subdue these . . . Apaches." The battalion then marched north, down the Santa Cruz River, reaching the Gila on December 21 and the Colorado on January 9. Rafts were constructed for fording the Colorado. One raft with Mormons aboard drifted into water too deep for the poles to reach bottom. Cooke, who was watching from the shore, shouted, "Try the other side [of the raft]." The men did, but the water there likewise was too deep for their poles to touch bottom. Cooke took off his hat, waved it at them, and called, "Goodbye, gentlemen! When you get down to the Gulf of California, give my respects to the folks!" And off he rode without a backward glance. Pushing across the desert of Southern California, the Mormon Battalion reached San Diego on January 29, 1847. There Cooke filed his official report, in which he stated, "Marching half naked and half fed, and living upon wild animals, we have discovered and made a road of great value to our country." Indeed they had, for Cooke's Wagon Road would be a major artery of traffic bound for the gold fields of California just three years later in the California gold rush of 1849.

One other detail of American soldiers marched through Arizona as a result of the Mexican War. Major Lawrence P. Graham was detailed to lead approximately five hundred troops from Monterrey, Mexico, to San Diego, California, in the summer of 1848. Their route of march was from Monterrey to Chihuahua City, Janos, San Bernardino, Tubac, Tucson, to the Gila and across to California. Lieutenant Cave J. Couts, who accompanied this march, wrote that Tubac contained a "small presidio" and that wealthy mines were being worked in the vicinity. "The Apaches are so numerous and severe," he wrote concerning this mining, "that the work only goes on at intervals, never over two weeks at a time." San Xavier mission he described as "truly a noble and stupendous building." But Tucson he found unimpressive: "Ft. de Tucson . . . the 2nd Chihuahua, is no *great deal* after all." Captain Comaduran came out to pay his respects this time, making no pretense of stopping the Americans, for the war officially had ended. Couts noted that every house in Tucson had a mill powered by burros that was kept running twenty-four hours a day, during which time half a bushel of wheat or corn could be ground into flour. The expedition then went on to the Gila and Colorado rivers, reaching San Diego on January 8, 1849.

The Mexican War was officially ended by the Treaty of Guadalupe Hidalgo, signed on February 2, 1848. It provided for the cession of a vast portion of Mexico to the United States for $15,000,000. Included in this cession was all of present Arizona north of the Gila River. This treaty was formally ratified on July 4, 1848, and seemingly restored peaceful relations between the two nations, but it contained seeds of discord. Specifically, the boundary of the Treaty of Guadalupe Hidalgo had to be surveyed and marked. This task proved to be far more difficult than had been anticipated.

THE BOUNDARY CONTROVERSY

In the fall of 1849 the first members of the United States Boundary Commission set foot on Arizona soil. Lieutenant Amiel Weeks Whipple, a member of the army's Corps of Topographical Engineers assigned to the commission, arrived at the junction of the Gila and Colorado rivers. His task was to survey the spot and to make maps of it. A native of Massachusetts and a graduate of West Point, Whipple had traversed the Southwest during the Mexican War, but he still found the raw frontier conditions not to his liking. Lieutenant Couts, commander of the dragoons protecting the surveyors, commented, "Poor Whipple! Times are hard on him. Ambulance, Umbrella. Oh My!"

But the lieutenant completed his work satisfactorily, and the boundary line dividing Lower and Upper California was established.

This work was performed under terms of Article V of the Treaty of Guadalupe Hidalgo. This article stipulated the new boundary and provided for a joint boundary commission with officials from both nations, whose task would be to run and mark the new boundary. The record of their acts, according to the treaty, would then become a part of the treaty and "have the same force as if it were inserted therein." Before leaving office in March, 1849, President James K. Polk appointed John B. Weller, an Ohio Democrat, as United States boundary commissioner and Andrew B. Gray of Texas as surveyor. They and their assistants met their Mexican counterparts in San Diego early in July of 1849 and in the next six months ran the line across Southern California. Meanwhile, the Whigs in the administration of Zachary Taylor had assumed office, and they began harassing the Democrat Weller by withholding funds for the survey. Unpaid personnel of the American commission began deserting for the gold fields, and the activities of hostile Indians in the area further hampered the work.

In September, 1849, word had arrived from Washington that Weller had been removed and the position of commissioner offered to John Charles Frémont. The "Great Pathfinder" at first accepted the post but resigned before actually assuming the office because he was elected to the United States Senate from California. Weller continued to serve until mid-February, 1850, when he was fired. At that time, because of the many difficulties encountered, the Joint Boundary Commission decided to adjourn after agreeing to meet again at El Paso del Norte (present

Juárez, Mexico) on the first Monday in November that same year. To complete the marking of the California boundary, the government appointed William H. Emory the temporary commissioner to complete the work on the Pacific Coast. Major Emory, also a member of the army's Corps of Topographical Engineers, and Surveyor Gray completed this task despite severe handicaps and hindrances, then made their way to Washington at personal expense, arriving in the capital on November 4, 1850. Emory was disgusted by what he considered the outrageous treatment at the hands of the government and asked to be relieved of further connection with the Joint Boundary Commission. Gray was ordered to resume his office with the commission, then in the field at El Paso del Norte.

Meanwhile a new commissioner had been appointed. After Frémont declined the permanent appointment, John Russell Bartlett, a New England Whig of scholarly inclinations, was appointed to the office. He was directed to proceed to El Paso by the nearest route in order to reach that community by November 1, if possible. Unaccustomed to government service—and actually incompetent to direct such work—Bartlett proceeded to make blunder after blunder. Political pressures led him to employ many workmen unsuited to the tasks, workmen who signed up only for the adventure they thought they might find.

Bartlett and the Mexican commissioner, General Pedro García Conde, held their first meeting on December 3, 1850. Thereupon they discovered a problem. Article V of the settlement at Guadalupe Hidalgo declared that the boundary would commence three marine leagues out in the Gulf of Mexico, proceed up the deepest channel of the Río Grande "to the point where it strikes the southern boundary of New Mexico; thence westwardly along the southern boundary of New Mexico (which runs north of a town called Paso) to its western termination; thence northward along the western line of New Mexico until it intersects the first branch of the River Gila." This southern boundary of New Mexico, the treaty stipulated, was to be as "laid down in the map entitled 'Map of the United Mexican States'" published by J. Disturnell at New York in 1847. Yet Bartlett and Conde discovered almost immediately that Disturnell's map was inaccurate. On this map the southern boundary of New Mexico was shown as being 8 miles above El Paso, then ran westward for 3° of longitude (or approximately 178 miles) before turning north to the nearest branch of the Gila. But the map showed El Paso at 32° 15′ north latitude, while its true position was 31° 45′. And the map showed the Río Grande at El Paso to be 104° 39′ west longitude, while its true position was 106° 29′. This error of half a degree in latitude placed El Paso 34 miles too far north and almost 100 miles too far east on Disturnell's map.

Conde argued that the position of El Paso on the treaty map must be followed. In short, he wanted the initial point of the boundary to begin 8 miles north of 32° 15′ north latitude—42 miles north of the actual location of El Paso, not 8 miles. And he wanted the 3° of longitude to begin at 104° 39′—which meant that the southern boundary of New Mexico would extend westward only about 120 miles before turning north, not 178 miles. Finally a compromise was reached. On Christmas Day, 1850, Conde and Bartlett decided that the Americans would allow the boundary to begin at 32° 22′ north latitude, while the Mexicans would allow it to run westward from that point a full 178 miles. Bartlett jubilantly wrote the secretary of the interior, his superior, that he had surrendered land of no value south of this initial point on the Río Grande while gaining land to the west that possibly contained copper, silver, and gold mines. But Surveyor Andrew B. Gray had not yet arrived on the scene, and the signature of the surveyor was necessary to the legal completion of the agreement. Bartlett therefore named Lieutenant Whipple Surveyor *Ad Interim*, he signed the document, and the survey westward from the Río Grande began 42 miles north of El Paso.

On June 24, 1851, Gray made his long delayed appearance at El Paso—and refused to agree to the Bartlett-Conde Agreement, stating that thereby Bartlett had given away six thousand square miles of territory belonging to the United States. Whipple's signature on the document was worthless, Gray asserted. Bartlett and Gray turned to the secretary of the interior to resolve their difference of opinion. Each sent long letters to Washington, believing that he would be upheld and his opponent reprimanded. But the mails were slow, and it would take months to learn the decision from Washington. Meanwhile the summer season was upon them, the time when the survey should proceed rapidly. While the decision from Washington was awaited, the survey of the Gila River could go forward safely, for on that point there was no contention. Bartlett therefore sent Surveyor Gray, Lieutenant Whipple, and an army escort, totaling forty-six men, to work on this river while he went south in search of supplies. Bartlett's trip into Mexico took him to Ures and Hermosillo, Sonora—even to Acapulco—where he boarded a boat that brought him to San Diego,

California, where he arrived on February 9, 1852. There he met Gray and Whipple and learned of the adventure that had befallen them.

On October 10, 1851, they had begun their work just below the San Carlos branch of the Gila, and by December 24 they had run and marked the boundary for 350 miles —to within 60 miles of the junction of the Gila with the Colorado. There they ran out of supplies and were forced to suspend the survey. Carefully marking the spot where they ended their work, they set out for San Diego. Arriving at the crossing of the Colorado, they found that Fort Yuma, an army post on the California side of the river, had been abandoned. In fact, rather than finding an army post, they were confronted at the crossing by an angry force of "1500 Indians, the flower of the Yuma nation." The Indians were in possession of the two flatboats used as the ferry, and the river was then a quarter of a mile wide and from fifteen to thirty feet deep. When informed that they could not cross, the Americans went into camp for the night. During the hours of darkness their interpreter overheard Yuma plans to massacre them. The soldiers and surveyors hastily erected a breastwork of their wagons and baggage. The next day, Christmas Day in fact, passed with no attack, the preparation of the Americans apparently causing the Indians to pause.

Toward nightfall Chief Azul and his leading warrior, known as Juan Antonio, approached the American camp. He wanted to know, he said through the interpreter, how much money the Americans had and where it was kept. Whipple responded that the Indians would be paid two dollars apiece to ferry the men across the Colorado and one dollar for each horse and mule. During the course of this interview, the families of the two chiefs wandered into the camp, apparently curious about the Americans. Suddenly a young Indian girl, fourteen or fifteen years of age, moved forward to whisper into the ear of her father, Juan Antonio. He in turn called Chief Azul aside and whispered to him. Other Indians wandered up and joined the mysterious conference, and as soon as they heard what was being said every eye was turned on Lieutenant Whipple. Finally the interpreter told Whipple, "These warriors think they have seen you before. They would like to know whether you came to the Colorado river from San Diego, on the Pacific coast, two years ago, and camped on the hill opposite this present camp."

Whipple replied affirmatively, and the young Indian maid arose and came forward with her father. "I saw by the expression of delight on the face of the interpreters," a member of the American group later wrote, "that all danger was past." The reason for the Indians' change of intentions soon became clear. When Whipple had been at the Colorado two years previously, surveying the junction of the rivers, he had found the Indian girl in a state of hunger and suffering in the desert to the west. He had taken her to his tent where he had given her a watermelon and, as a present, a small mirror before returning her safely to her home. She had not forgotten the favor, and within an hour the Yumas were busy ferrying the surveying party across the river.

Reunited at San Diego, the American Boundary Survey Commission began its return trip. As they journeyed across Arizona, they paused to complete the survey of the Gila River, then pushed across New Mexico to El Paso. There they learned the result of the quarrel between Bartlett and Gray over the Bartlett-Conde Agreement. Gray had been removed by the secretary of the interior and had been replaced as surveyor by Major William H. Emory. Emory had arrived at El Paso on November 25, 1851, to find Bartlett and Gray gone west and those members of the commission remaining demoralized and disorganized. He put them to work surveying the Río Grande. When Bartlett returned, he found Emory at Ringgold Barracks, Texas, only 241 miles from the mouth of the Río Grande. There, just before Christmas of 1852, Bartlett was reunited with his surveying party—and there he received word from Washington to suspend work.

Since 1849, Congress from time to time had taken notice of the survey because of the many complaints that had been lodged against Bartlett. John B. Weller, the first commissioner, had been elected to the United States Senate from California after he was removed from the boundary survey team, and he had used his new position to criticize the work of his replacement. Other persons likewise had advanced charges against Bartlett, so that by the summer of 1852 he stood charged with making private use of government transportation, of unpardonable mismanagement of public funds, of disregard for the health, comfort, and safety of those under him, and of general negligence. But it was the Bartlett-Conde Agreement that most discredited the commissioner. Southerners, especially Texans, were indignant at this compromise, for the six thousand square miles of territory that Bartlett had signed away were vitally necessary for the construction of a southern transcontinental railroad (and the region at the eastern end of a transcontinental railroad would profit tremendously). Bartlett's critics were able to attach a rider to the deficiency appropriations bill of 1852, as well as to the appropriations bill for fiscal 1852–53, to the effect that none of the money for the boundary survey could be spent to run and mark a line farther north of the town of El Paso than shown on the treaty map. The administration of Millard Fillmore had no recourse but to halt the survey. Bartlett sold the field equipment and the commission's animals in San Antonio, disbanded the crews in his employ, and retired from the field. The survey of Arizona's southern boundary had come to a halt.

Political maneuvering over the boundary had just begun, however. Governor William Carr Lane of New Mexico believed the six thousand square miles in dispute to be under his jurisdiction and insisted that he would exercise control over it. Governor Angél Trias of Chihuahua believed the opposite. He declared that the Bartlett-Conde Agreement was legal, and he moved troops into the region along with a proclamation that he would fight for it. However, the five hundred men that Trias sent could not be supplied and had to be withdrawn to El Paso. Governor Lane organized a force of New Mexican and Texan volunteers and marched to the village of Doña Ana, where he issued a proclamation claiming the Mesilla Valley for the United States. A second Mexican War seemed imminent. Any small incident would have touched off shooting.

At this critical juncture both the United States and Mexico took a long second look at the situation. Newly inaugurated President Franklin Pierce knew that the first Mexican War had badly divided the country; another would surely be bad for the country—as well as harmful for the Democratic party. In Mexico the recently returned dictator, Antonio López de Santa Anna, desperately needed money, not another war with the United States. With both sides favoring a peaceful resolution of the dispute, a solution was found. In March, 1853, President Pierce sent James Gadsden of South Carolina to Mexico with orders to settle all areas of dispute between the two nations. The result was the treaty that bears Gadsden's name. On December 30, 1853, the Gadsden Purchase agreement was signed. It provided, as finally ratified by the United States Senate, for payment of $10,000,000 to Mexico in return for the area known as the Gadsden Purchase—in short, the present international boundary. Major William H. Emory was appointed the new boundary commissioner, and by the summer of 1855 the limits between the two nations had been run and marked. All of the present Arizona thereby had become American territory.

That part of Arizona within the Gadsden Purchase, as well as that part of the present state that was included in the Mexican Cession, was attached to the Territory of New Mexico. This territory, created in 1850 by Congress, included all of present Arizona and New Mexico, as well as a portion of Nevada and Colorado. But the Mexican garrison at Tucson commanded by Captain Hilarion García did not leave the Old Pueblo until March of 1856. Americans already there, along with the older residents, loudly protested the withdrawal of the Mexican troops, for no American soldiers had yet arrived, and they were thus exposed to Apache wrath and raids. Not until November 14, 1856, did Major Enoch Steen with three companies of the First Dragoons arrive at Tucson to unfurl the Stars and Stripes. Arizona at last had come under American military protection. Arizona as a separate entity did not yet exist. Santa Fe, the capital of New Mexico, was far removed, and the population was scant, but Arizona was American—and in the hills and moun-

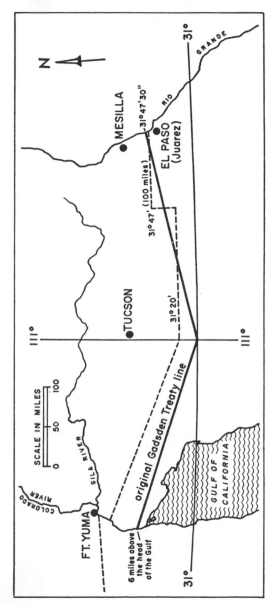

The Gadsden Purchase, showing the line as originally drawn and as changed in the United States Senate. *Drawn by Don Bufkin*

tains was mineral wealth sufficient to attract restless, adventuresome men to settle the rugged land.

THE COMING OF THE ANGLOS

Lieutenant Cave J. Couts, who commanded the military escort for Whipple's survey of the junction of the Gila and Colorado rivers, commented on the first major group of Americans to enter Arizona following the Mexican War—the forty-niners: "My table admits of but three seats, and upon several occasions, I have not got in before the 4th table, very frequently having to keep it set from three P.M., until eight or nine o'clock at night, and then direct the cook to say that the provisions are out, and that the commissary Sergt. is absent. From the way they shovel down the pork and bread, is sufficient proof of its rarity, and sugar and coffee! Some are worse than ratholes to fill." Not only were these gold-seekers hungry; most of them were half-lost. "They . . . are willing," wrote Couts, "to keep me talking and making way-bills for them from sun-up to sun-down and from sun-down to sun-up."

As indicated by Couts's comments, thousands were crossing the continent to the new El Dorado in 1849. Many of these forty-niners chose to cross by the southern route, originally called Cooke's Wagon Road but renamed the Gila Trail during the gold rush; approximately nine thousand Americans followed this route in 1849 alone, while in the period 1849–51 inclusive some sixty thousand came across it. This route was popular because there were fewer mountains to cross, and the weather, while hot, was more tolerable than summer sun and wintry cold to the north. Also there were several Mexican villages along the way where food and other supplies could be purchased: corn, barley, eggs, dried beef, and, as one pilgrim wrote, "miserable coffee." Obviously some women were in these parties of pioneers, for in 1849 as one group drifted down the Gila River on rafts the first American child was born in Arizona; reportedly he was named Gila Howard.

As most of these parties of forty-niners were large, they were not molested by the Indians. Individuals or families foolish enough to try to cross in small numbers were frequently victims of Indian attack. For example, the Oatman family arrived in Tucson in January, 1850, in company with a large wagon train. Almost all of the others voted to rest in the Old Pueblo, but three families, including the Oatmans, chose to push on. Arriving at the Pima villages on the Gila River on February 16, the party halted. The other two families chose to remain there until a wagon train should come along to provide the safety of numbers, but the Oatmans chose to cross alone. On the evening of March 19, 1850, the family was encamped on the banks of the Gila River some 118 miles east of Yuma. That evening the father was depressed, declaring, "I know something dreadful is about to happen." He was right. Early the next morning nineteen Yavapai Indians rode up demanding food. Oatman truthfully replied that he had little to eat. The Indians grew angry and with clubs killed Oatman, his wife, and their three youngest children. Lorenzo, an older boy, was clubbed and thrown over a cliff for dead, while Olive Oatman, age twelve, and Mary, age eight, were made captives and forced to accompany the Indians. Lorenzo later recovered consciousness, was picked up by a passing wagon train, and taken to Fort Yuma, an army post established late in 1849 on the California side of the Colorado River to protect these goldseekers. At Fort Yuma Lorenzo told his story and tried to interest the soldiers in recovering his sisters, but the troops were too few in number to ride on this mission. Lorenzo moved to Los Angeles, California, where for five years he sought aid in rescuing his sisters.

Meanwhile Olive and Mary were traded by the Yavapais to the Mohave Indians, under whose cruel treatment Mary died. Olive lived despite being tattooed in Mohave fashion and being forced to perform menial tasks. Finally, in January of 1856, Henry Grinnell, a carpenter at Fort Yuma, heard of the female captive of the Mohaves from Francisco, a Yuma Indian. Grinnell feigned knowledge of this, picked up a Los Angeles newspaper, and, seemingly reading, concocted a story to the effect that a large body of armed Americans were coming to punish the Mohaves. Francisco was impressed, but was much more interested in Grinnell's comment that a liberal reward would go to Olive Oatman's rescuer. The Yuma warrior promised he would bring the girl to Fort Yuma—and he did. He secured her release by trade and by making the Mohaves believe they were shortly to be punished for holding Olive captive. Olive was incoherent for several days after her rescue and then could speak only haltingly about her ordeal. Lorenzo was notified of his sister's rescue, rode to Fort Yuma for a tearful reunion, and then moved her to Oregon.

Some of the forty-niners using the Gila route to the gold fields more than repaid the Indians for their few raids on American parties. A few of the more adventurous "Argonauts" chose to become scalp bounty hunters for the states of Chihuahua and Sonora. By 1849 these bounties had risen to the munificent sum of $200 for a warrior's scalp and $100 for that of a squaw or child. Prominent among those engaged in such "backyard barbering" were Michael James Box, James Kirker, James Johnson, and John Joel

Glanton. Glanton was operating first in the state of Chihuahua but had to flee it when he was discovered turning in the scalps of Mexicans for the bounties. With a price tag of $8,000 on his own scalp, Glanton took his followers to Sonora. One pass through the countryside netted over $6,500 in bounty money. Then he transferred his activities to Arizona. At Yuma Crossing he found the Yuma Indians operating a very profitable ferry service for gold-seekers. Glanton and his gang saw the potential of this operation and took it over by force. The Yumas suffered in silence for a time, then on April 23, 1850, attacked the Glanton gang and killed fifteen of them. Among the dead was Glanton himself, who died by the scalp as he had lived by it. A few survivors made their way to Los Angeles, where they told of a "Yuma massacre." The state of California sent a small army of volunteers, under the command of state Adjutant General Joseph G. Morehead. The Yumas easily repulsed the Californians, however.

The Yumas had not been protected by soldiers from Fort Yuma, nor were Glanton and his men aided from the same source, because Fort Yuma temporarily had been abandoned. Originally established in 1849, this post first was called Camp Calhoun. It was named Camp Independence in 1850 and as such operated until March of 1851, when it was abandoned. It was reoccupied in February of 1852 by troops commanded by Major Samuel P. Heintzelman, at which time it was given the designation Fort Yuma. Other military installations in Arizona prior to the Civil War included Fort Buchanan, established by the dragoons who came to Tucson in November, 1856, under the command of Major Enoch Steen; Fort Defiance, founded in northeastern Arizona in 1852 (present Apache County) for control of the Navahos; Fort Mohave, first called Camp Colorado, which was established in 1859 on the Colorado River at approximately the thirty-fifth parallel to protect immigrants to California; Fort Aravaipa, later called Fort Breckenridge, which was founded in 1860 at the junction of the Aravaipa and San Pedro rivers and intended as a deterrent to Apache raiding parties; and Camp Tucson, also established in 1860. All of these military posts were controlled either by the Departments of New Mexico or California, for as yet there was no territory called Arizona.

As to civil government, there was little or none. Technically Arizona was part of the Territory of New Mexico, created by Congress in 1850. The legislature of that territory simply extended its county lines westward to California. For example, Socorro County included all the present Salt River Valley region, while Doña Ana County became the largest county in the territory after the Gadsden Purchase. But these counties had neither the money nor the inclination to exercise any real control over their far western parts. Thus it was left to the initiative of the local settlements to provide their own government, and there were few such villages. Tucson remained largely a Mexican villa with few Anglo-American settlers. Tubac, to the south of Tucson, was virtually abandoned. One new village was created on the banks of the Colorado River across from Fort Yuma. First called Colorado City, then Arizona City, it eventually took the name Yuma, and so it remains.

Connecting these forts and towns were a few scattered trails. Roads were desperately needed, especially to supply the army posts, and means of transportation of people, supplies, and the mail had to be created. Leading the vanguard of those seeking such routes were members of the army Corps of Topographical Engineers. Between September and December of 1851, Captain Lorenzo Sitgreaves led a party of twenty men from the Zuñi Indian villages of New Mexico across Arizona by a route where the cities of Flagstaff, Williams, and Kingman later would be built (that is, approximately along the thirty-fifth parallel). At the Colorado River he turned south to Fort Yuma. Two years later Lieutenants Amiel Weeks Whipple and Joseph Christmas Ives were assigned the task of a railroad survey from Fort Smith, Arkansas, to Los Angeles, California. On this trek they followed much the same route as Sitgreaves, the thirty-fifth parallel. Then in 1854, following the Gadsden Purchase, Lieutenants John G. Parke and George Stoneman were assigned to survey a railroad route across the thirty-second parallel. Traveling from west to east, they entered Arizona at Fort Yuma, went to the Pima villages by way of the Gila, turned south to Tucson, and proceeded east along Cooke's Wagon Road. Finally, one civilian enterprise resulted in a survey across Arizona. The Texas Western Railroad Company, chartered by the state of Texas, commissioned Andrew B. Gray to survey for a thirty-second parallel railroad route, which he did in 1854, meeting Parke en route. As a result of such activities, the first accurate maps of Arizona were executed, and much of its geography became known.

A bizarre experiment led to a later survey along the thirty-fifth parallel. Naval Lieutenant Edward Fitzgerald Beale, a veteran of the Mexican War, undertook the opening of a wagon road along the thirty-fifth parallel. What made his attempt unique was his use of camels for transportation. Beale had conceived the idea that goods—even the mail—could best be moved across the American deserts by camels, and he found a supporter in Jefferson Davis, secretary of war in the Franklin Pierce administration. Supplies had been slow in reaching southwestern military posts, and their transportation had proved expensive. Davis, in December, 1853, urged Congressional action to establish a Camel Military Corps, declaring, "For military purposes, for expresses, and for reconnoissances, it is believed, the dromedary would supply a want now seriously felt in our service." Congress responded with an appropriation of $30,000 to import the animals.

Under Beale's direction, thirty-three Bactrian camels reached Indianola, Texas, in 1856. The following year another forty-four camels arrived, and all were located at Camp Verde, Texas (sixty miles northwest of San Antonio). Two drivers from Egypt were imported to train soldiers in packing the animals. Their names seemed unpronounceable to Americans and were soon corrupted into "Greek George" and "Hi-Jolly." Beale departed Camp Verde on June 25, 1857, each camel carrying six to eight hundred pounds and traveling twenty-five to thirty miles a day. By August they were at the Zuñi Indian villages, ready to enter Arizona. That crossing was completed by January, 1858, when they reached the Colorado. The return to Texas was uneventful, after which Beale wrote a report to the secretary of war about the camel's abilities: "The harder the test they are put to, the more fully they seem to justify all that can be said of them. They pack water for others four days under a hot sun and never get a drop; they pack heavy burdens of corn and oats for months and never get a grain; and on the bitter greasewood and other worthless shrubs not only subsist but keep fat." He concluded, "I look forward to the day when every

mail route across the continent will be conducted and
worked altogether with this economical and noble brute."

Beale's optimistic evaluation was reflected by Secretary
of War John B. Floyd, who in 1858 reported to Congress,
"The entire adaptation of camels to military operations
on the plains may now be taken as demonstrated." He
recommended that Congress authorize the purchase of
one thousand camels at once. Again in 1859 and in 1860
he made the same recommendation, but the lawmakers
were concerned with the rising sectional controversy, not
with camels. Therefore no new beasts were purchased.
The seventy-seven already in the country were employed
in various tasks during these years, however. Beale used
twenty of them on surveying expeditions and road construction in the Southwest, while other officers supervised
the use of the remainder. All reports were enthusiastic.
But with the opening shots of the Civil War, the Camel
Military Corps was disbanded and the beasts sold at public
auction. Some were bought to pack ore in Arizona, others
to pack salt in Nevada. A few escaped to run wild in the
desert where they were shot on sight by prospectors and
hunters, who regarded them as pests and nuisances.

When Edward Fitzgerald Beale arrived at the Colorado
River in January, 1858, with his camels, he encountered
what to him was a strange sight—a steamboat. The men
aboard the ship doubtless were just as astonished to see
camels approaching the river. Both were pioneering new
forms of transportation in Arizona, but the steamboat
would prove of more lasting benefit. The first steamboat
on the Colorado came as a result of the establishment of
Fort Yuma. Supplies intended for that post had to be
freighted by wagon over what one officer declared to be

a desert "as hazardous and pernicious as so much Sahara or Gobi." The cost of bringing one ton of supplies by wagon from San Diego was from $500 to $800 per ton. Cheaper means had to be found. Major General Persifor F. Smith, commanding the Division of the Pacific, in the fall of 1850 ordered Lieutenant George H. Derby to determine the navigability of the Colorado. Derby, already famous for his humorous writings under the names John Phoenix and "The Veritable Squibob," sailed from San Francisco aboard the 120-ton schooner *Invincible*. Rounding the tip of Baja California, the ship passed through the Gulf of California and entered the Colorado River on December 24. Then, using a small boat, Derby rowed upstream to a point eighty miles below Fort Yuma, where he met Major Heintzelman. His report of this effort stressed that boats of a shallow draft could easily reach Yuma. Thereby he opened the door to steam navigation of the Colorado, a feat for which he is not generally remembered. Southwesterners usually recall him as a humorist— and there is something appealing about a man who could write that he never saw a bald head without wanting to decorate it with a map of the Chinese Empire.

Shortly after Derby's report was published, the army awarded a contract to Captain George Alonso Johnson to undertake the supplying of Fort Yuma by water. Johnson brought freight to the mouth of the Colorado by ocean-going vessels, then transferred the goods to a fifty-foot barge which was poled upriver. Indian attacks and the difficulty of using manpower against the stiff current of the Colorado proved this experiment unsatisfactory, however, and Johnson terminated his contract. Early in 1852, Captain James Turnbull accepted the challenge. He bought the *Uncle Sam*, a twenty-horsepower stern-wheeler which measured sixty-five feet and had a draft of only twenty-two inches. The craft was assembled and launched at the mouth of the Colorado, and it made the run to Fort Yuma easily, despite the current. Turnbull did not have problems with the Indians, for they ran from his vessel, shouting "The devil is coming, blowing fire and smoke out of his nose and kicking the water back with his feet." Later, their fear overcome by familiarity, the natives cut wood and sold it to the captain at designated points along the river.

In 1853, Turnbull's contract was terminated, and once again George A. Johnson was awarded the right to supply the army's needs at Fort Yuma. Johnson was joined by others in the venture, and the firm was designated George A. Johnson and Company. Larger boats were brought to the Colorado, such as the *Colorado*, a 120-foot stern-wheeler capable of towing two barges. The next advance came in 1857, the year that President James Buchanan was confronted with the so-called "Mormon War." An army expedition under the command of Colonel Albert S. Johnston was dispatched to Utah with the purpose of enforcing stricter compliance with federal statutes and stricter obedience to federal officials. This army had to be supplied, and the cheapest means would be by water. Therefore federal funds became available for exploration of the Colorado River above Fort Yuma to determine how far north it was navigable. George A. Johnson, when asked, replied that he wanted $3,500 per month to charter the *Colorado* for this purpose. Secretary of War Jefferson Davis considered this too expensive and sought other means of exploring the river. Johnson, however, was so determined to be first up the river that he conducted his own expedition without federal funding. In the *Colorado* he ascended the river to Black Canyon (near the present Hoover Dam) and returned to Yuma; it was on this trip that he encountered Beale and the camels.

Johnson's expedition was shortly followed by a government survey. A vessel, the *Explorer*, was constructed at Philadelphia, disassembled, transported to the mouth of the Colorado, and there reassembled. Then, with Lieutenant Joseph Christmas Ives of the Topographical Engineers in command, it started upriver on December 21, 1857. Nineteen days later it was at Fort Yuma. After a short rest there, Ives proceeded upriver and on March 12 reached Black Canyon. There he was stopped, just as Johnson had been halted. After his return to Fort Yuma, he reported that Black Canyon was the head of navigation on the Colorado. Just downriver from Black Canyon, William H. Hardy established Hardyville in 1864 and grew rich from the passage of goods at his landing at the head of steamer navigation.

Both camels and steamboats were too limited for the general passenger and freighting needs of Arizona, however. Camels were used only on an experimental basis, and steamboats ran only on the Colorado. Desperately needed was some means of conveying people and the mail —if not freight—to their destination. Especially was this true for California, where there was a growing clamor for transcontinental mail service. Congress responded to this clamor by subsidizing a stage line to run from the end of railroad track in the East to the Pacific Coast. Such a run had to be twice weekly, and it had to make the run in twenty-five days or less. Furthermore, it had to begin service within a year of the signing of the contract. During this one-year interim, Congress subsidized a monthly mail service from San Antonio to San Diego. Californian

James Birch was paid $150,000 to operate what he named officially the San Antonio and San Diego Mail Line, but what became popularly known as the "Jackass Mail" because certain sections of its route were so unfit for wheeled vehicles that the passengers were forced to ride mules.

The Jackass Mail died a quiet death when the larger undertaking began operating in 1858. Postmaster General Aaron Brown had signed a contract on September 16, 1857, with John Butterfield and Associates to operate the twice-weekly stage, and thus the line became known as the Butterfield Overland Mail. Butterfield, a man with years of experience in the staging business and one of the founders of the American Express Company, did what he was told was impossible. In just one year he had hired personnel, acquired horses, mules, and stages, and was ready to begin service on September 16, 1858. That day, from both Tipton, Missouri, and San Francisco, California, stages began rolling west and east, as they would twice weekly thereafter from each terminus. The route was from Tipton, a railhead town, to Fort Smith, Arkansas, thence across Texas by way of a string of forts (Griffin, Chadbourne, and Davis) to El Paso, north to Mesilla, New Mexico, west to Tucson and Yuma, on to Los Angeles, and finally to San Francisco. Waterman L. Ormsby, a reporter for the New York *Herald*, made the first trip west from Tipton, riding all the way to San Francisco. Along the way he filed dispatches to his paper telling of his experiences.

The stage station at which he first stopped in Arizona, to eat a hasty meal of beans, fried salt pork, and coffee, was Stein's Peak. Other stations in Arizona included Apache Pass, Dragoon Springs, Cienega, Tucson, Point-of-Mountain, Picacho Pass, Sacaton, Maricopa Wells, Gila Ranch, Murderer's Grave, Flap-Jack Ranch, Peterman's Filibuster

Camp, Snively's Ranch, and Yuma. "Tucson," wrote Ormsby, "is a small place, consisting of a few adobe houses. The inhabitants are mainly Mexicans. There are but few Americans, though they keep the two or three stores and are elected to the town offices. The town has considerably improved since the acquisition of the territory by the United States."

Passengers on the Butterfield were expected to aid in repelling Indian raiders, to push the stage when it became stuck or when going up a steep hill, and to give general help in any emergency. Sitting upright on stages without springs, they rode night and day for the twenty-four days it took to make the trip from Missouri to California—for which they paid a fare of $200. But the Butterfield did provide passenger and mail service to Arizona, and it opened the region somewhat to the outside world. By stage, steamboat, horseback, afoot, and even on camels, Americans were moving to the territory.

New Settlers

Following the American acquisition of Arizona, the first new settlers came principally in the hope of wresting quick wealth from the land. A few such pioneers did intend to settle permanently, to farm, ranch, or operate stores, but primarily it was Arizona's mineral potential that lured men to what to them seemed a hard, harsh country. Desert heat and aridity, along with Indian raiders, induced little settlement, but gold and silver did. Coming to Arizona first in search of precious metals was the man who would do much to achieve separate territorial status for it, Charles Debrille Poston.

A native of Kentucky, Poston in 1850, at the age of twenty-five, moved to San Francisco, where he became chief clerk in the surveyor's office at the customs house. When news of the impending Gadsden Purchase reached that city late in 1853, Poston became very excited and was easily persuaded by a French syndicate to lead an expedition to the area in search of silver. Recruiting some twenty-five men, Poston sailed for Guaymas, Sonora, in February, 1854, on the British ship *Zoraida*. Unfortunately the *Zoraida* was shipwrecked in the Gulf of California on the coast of the Mexican state Sinaloa, but Poston and his men reached shore safely. Then they marched northward, up through Sinaloa and Sonora into southern Arizona. South of Tucson they did find rich probability of silver. Then they went north to Tucson and the Gila River, which they followed to Fort Yuma. At Yuma, Poston met Major Samuel P. Heintzelman, commanding officer at the post, and they excitedly discussed the possibilities. Poston then went to California to report to the French syndicate, after which he journeyed to Cincinnati, Ohio—Heintzelman's home town—where the Sonora Exploring and Mining Company was capitalized at one million dollars, $100,000 paid in. The new firm was established with Heintzelman as president. Poston, as general manager, had orders to hire employees and establish mines in Arizona. He recruited these followers in San Antonio, men he later described as "armed with Sharp's rifles, Colt's revolvers, and the recklessness of youth."

Poston brought this crew to the old Spanish garrison of Tubac, which had been abandoned when the Mexican troops left Arizona in early 1856. Poston found that, though the doors and windows had been removed, the buildings were habitable. The commanding officers' quarters became the company headquarters, while the barracks became rooms for the men. The old guardhouse afforded ample storeroom for company property. And the tower, three stories of which were still standing, was ideal for posting a sentry to watch for marauding Apaches. Poston sent men to the Santa Rita Mountains for timber to make doors and windows, and soon Tubac was in good physical condition again. Supplies were easily obtained. Wild game —quail, ducks, antelope, and deer—abounded in the vicinity, so that even a poor hunter could keep the dining table well supplied with meat. Poston hired a German gardener who fenced and cultivated fields with irrigation water from the Santa Cruz River. At nearby Tumacacori, the abandoned mission, the orchards planted by the padres still were bearing fruit. Beef, flour, beans, sugar, and coffee could be obtained from Sonora at reasonable prices. Poston even had his men dig deep pools in the Santa Cruz. These pools were shaded by trees, and there, according to one witness, Poston "used to sit in the water, like the Englishman in *Hyperion*, and read the newspapers, by which means he kept his temper cool amid the various disturbing influences that surrounded him." Of this period at Tubac, where civil officials from New Mexico were unknown, Poston later reminisced, "We had no law but love, and no occupation but labor. No government, no taxes, no public debt, no politics. It was a community in a perfect state of nature."

And the company prospered financially. Several mines were developed, the richest called the Heintzelman. This mine had been worked in Spanish-Mexican days, when it was called the Cerro Colorado, and under Poston's supervision was made to produce handsomely. In 1859 the company bought a European barrel amalgamating works in San Francisco for $39,000. This was brought by water to Yuma, then overland to Tubac where it was erected near the Heintzelman. Soon some $3,000 a day in silver was coming from it. Poston was canny enough to ship ore by wagon to various cities in the East for assay; these reports invariably caused investment in the Sonora Exploring and Mining Company. Poston wrote, "Upon the arrival of these ores in the States, they were distributed to the different cities for examination and assay and gave the country [Arizona] its first reputation as a producer of minerals."

Another promoter of mining activity in Arizona prior to the Civil War was Sylvester Mowry, a Rhode Island graduate of the Military Academy who was assigned to Fort Yuma in 1855. Duty there was not to his liking. He wrote in a letter to a friend in April, 1856, that the weather was unbearably hot, that the post was far from civilization, and that he was bored with drilling troops; the principal occupation of the officers, he said, was drinking ale. When he heard of a meeting in Tucson for the purpose of seeking separate territorial status for Arizona, he saw it as a means of escape. Actually, the meeting in Tucson was not the first such effort to separate from New Mexico but the second. The United States attorney for New Mexico, William C. Jones, had called a meeting in Mesilla, New Mexico (present Las Cruces), during the summer of 1856. A petition to Congress resulted, signed by fifty-seven persons, requesting that Arizona be separated from New Mexico along the thirty-fourth parallel (that is, that present Arizona and New Mexico be separated by a line running east-west along the thirty-fourth parallel, as opposed to the present separation by a north-south line). At the urging of Poston, the name Arizona was used for this proposed territory. Then in Tucson in August, 1856, Poston also participated in the meeting of which Mowry heard. The convention in Tucson like-wise petitioned Congress to separate Arizona from New Mexico, protesting that Arizonans had no law, no courts, no vote, and no representation in any legislative body. Their petition bore 260 signatures—a revealing list of the pioneers of Arizona: Mark Aldrich, the first Anglo-American merchant in Tucson; Herman Ehrenberg, a German immigrant and cartographer; Edward E. Dunbar, who operated the copper mines at Ajo; Peter R. Brady, later a sheriff of Pima County; and Frederick A. Ronstadt, Granville Oury, Charles Schuchard (the artist), and others who would influence the course of Arizona's destiny. This petition subsequently was introduced in Congress by Miguel A. Otero, the territorial representative from New Mexico, but nothing came of it.

Mowry, when he heard of this convention, decided that Arizona indeed should be a separate territory and that he should represent it in Congress. On May 15, 1857, he took sick leave from the army and set out for Washington with fresh proposals for a Territory of Arizona. While in the capital that fall he advised John Butterfield on operating a stage line through Arizona, and he wrote and had printed a pamphlet entitled *Memoir on the Proposed Territory of Arizona*, the first published work devoted exclusively to Arizona. Mowry also, while in the East, organized the Arizona Land and Mining Company, which bought the Sopori Grant, a Spanish land grant, containing some 220 square miles. The former boundary commissioner, John R. Bartlett, wrote the prospectus for this company and invested in it.

By July of 1858, Mowry had become so involved in business that he resigned his commission in the army. Returning to Arizona, he was re-elected territorial delegate (still without a seat in Congress, however). In February, 1859, while again in Washington, he was appointed to head a survey of the Pima and Maricopa Indian lands and to distribute presents to them. That summer in Arizona, carrying out this assignment, he became involved in an argument with Edward E. Cross, editor of the first newspaper in Arizona, the Tubac *Weekly Arizonian.* Cross had written that Mowry was exaggerating the beauties of the territory in order to attract investors. Feeling he had been called a liar, Mowry demanded satisfaction. They fought with Burnside rifles at forty paces. Each missed several times before Mowry said he was satisfied. The two men then shook hands, after which they adjourned to a nearby saloon and broke open a forty-two-gallon barrel of whisky. The beverage, wrote Mowry later, "melted before the fierce attacks like snow before the midday sun." Shortly thereafter Mowry purchased the *Weekly Arizonian,* moved it to Tucson, and published it subsequently as a Democratic party organ for the territory.

By the end of 1859, Mowry had completed his survey of the Pima and Maricopa reservations and had distributed presents to these Indians. In April, 1860, he was asked again to serve as Arizona's representative to Congress, but ten bills to create a territory had failed passage, and Mowry declined, deciding to devote his energies to mining. On April 9, 1860, he acquired title to what had been known as the Patagonia Mine for $22,500. He changed the name to the Mowry Mine, and soon it was a steady producer of silver.

One other area of mining activity became prominent in Arizona prior to the Civil War. To the west, where Juan de Oñate had heard tales of gold in 1604, gold was discovered. Jacob Snively, a Texas veteran of the Mexican

War, struck pay dirt on the Gila River some twenty miles upstream from Yuma, and Gila City was born. The strike reportedly was so rich that an inexperienced miner could work twenty dollars of gold from eight shovelfuls of dirt. By 1861 some twelve hundred miners were there. A traveler declared, "The earth was turned inside out. . . . Enterprising men hurried to the spot with barrels of whiskey and billiard tables; . . . traders crowded in with wagonloads of pork and beans; and gamblers came with cards and monte tables. There was everything in Gila City within a few months but a church and a jail, which were accounted barbarisms by the mass of the population." But the gold in the stream bed soon was exhausted, and by 1864 Gila City was a ghost town. That year another visitor wrote that "the promising Metropolis of Arizona consisted of three chimneys and a coyote."

Not all who moved to Arizona in the 1850's came to mine, however. At Yuma was L. J. F. Jaeger (also spelled Iager), a native of Pennsylvania who came to Yuma in 1850 with riverboat captain George A. Johnson. Buying out the owner of the ferry across the Colorado, Jaeger prospered from moving men and supplies across the river. Next he invested in mines in the vicinity and expanded into the freighting business, supplying hay to the army at $60 a ton. In short, he became rich. Others who moved to Arizona came because of the agricultural potential, men such as Pete Kitchen. Arriving in southern Arizona in 1854, he established a ranch and farm seven miles north of present Nogales. Unfortunately he had located astride an Apache war trail, and thus his home became a fortress. He built an adobe house, topped by a flat roof sporting a parapet three to four feet high, and always kept a sentinel there to sound the alarm when the Indians were seen.

Indians liked to stop at his ranch. The Apaches had long familiarity with cattle, but Kitchen's large herd of pigs intrigued them. They shot arrows into his hogs until, said Kitchen, they looked like "perambulating pincushions."

This hardy farmer also had to contend with bandits from Sonora, but he soon taught them, as he taught the Apaches, to respect his deadly marksmanship with a rifle and his willingness to track them hundreds of miles to recover his property. Employing Opata Indians and Mexicans to work his thousands of acres and to herd his pigs and cattle, he marketed grain, potatoes, cabbage, fruit, and melons. From El Paso to Fort Yuma, stores boasted signs that they sold Kitchen's ham, bacon, and lard. Such enterprise soon made him wealthy by frontier standards.

Thus by the late 1850's Arizona had become a land of considerable enterprise. Army posts had been established. The government was subsidizing mail—and thereby stagecoach—service. Steamers were operating on the Colorado bringing supplies from the outside world at reasonable cost. Tucson was a city of activity. And Arizona's mines were giving the territory a fair reputation. Even the Indians thus far had been peaceful toward Americans. Charles D. Poston wrote that until 1860 the natives "had not . . . given us any trouble; but on the contrary, passed within sight of our herds, going hundreds of miles into Mexico on their forays rather than break their treaty with the Americans." But the favorable progress of Arizona during the 1850's was slowed and then reversed by events in 1860–61: the outbreak of hostilities with the Indians and the beginning of the Civil War.

Late in 1860 a group of twenty-five to thirty Mexicans came to Poston's headquarters at Tubac with information that Apaches had raided their ranches in Sonora and had stolen some three hundred head of horses and mules. The Mexicans further stated that the Apaches were headed toward a crossing of the Santa Cruz River between Canoa and Tucson. The Mexicans asked Poston and his men to aid in laying an ambush for the Indians, promising in return to give the Americans half the animals recovered. When Poston declined, the Mexicans rode to Canoa, an encampment of lumbermen from Maine, and made them the same offer. They accepted, and the ambush succeeded. The Apaches were caught in a murderous crossfire and abandoned the stock.

"About the next full moon after this event," later recalled Poston, "we had been passing the usual quiet Sunday at Tubac, when a Mexican vaquero came galloping furiously into the plaza crying out, 'Apaches! Apaches! Apaches!'" Poston learned from this man that the Apaches had attacked the lumberjacks in retaliation for their participation in the ambush. Poston gathered men and rushed to the lumbermen's camp—to be greeted by a scene of massacre and destruction. Doors and windows had been smashed, and the house was a smoking ruin. "The former inmates were lying around dead, and three of them had been thrown into the well, head foremost," wrote Poston. Soldiers from Fort Buchanan pursued the marauders but never caught the guilty ones.

Despite this incident, the Apaches remained on friendly terms with the majority of Americans—until an even more tragic occurrence changed their attitude. John Ward, a rancher living in the Sonoita Valley, triggered what came to be called the "Bascom Affair." Ward lived with his common-law wife, a former captive of the Apaches, and a stepson, Mickey Free, who had been sired during his mother's captivity. One day while drunk, Ward beat the boy so badly that he ran away. Then, still drunk, Ward went to Fort Buchanan to complain to the commanding officer that Cochise, chief of the Chiricahua Apaches, had stolen his stepson and some cattle. In January, 1861, Lieutenant George N. Bascom and fifty-four soldiers were sent to recover the boy and the cattle from Cochise. Ward went with them. Bascom's orders were to demand the return of the boy and the cattle—and to use force if necessary to attain his objective.

These troops reached Apache Pass, where Cochise was known to live, on February 3. Bascom led his troops past the Butterfield stage station and encamped three-quarters of a mile to the east. There the troops pitched camp and waited. The next day Cochise came into the camp with other curious Apaches, unaware of any danger. The Chiricahua chief along with seven other Apaches, mostly his relatives, entered Bascom's tent, which was then surrounded by soldiers. Bascom, through an interpreter, demanded that the boy and cattle be returned. When Cochise said he did not have them, Bascom replied that the chief and his party would be held hostages until the stock and the lad were returned. Once Cochise fully understood his situation, he drew a knife, slit a hole in the tent, and jumped out. He landed in the midst of startled soldiers, dashed through them before they could recover, and made his escape. A warrior who followed behind Cochise was clubbed and bayoneted. The remaining six Apaches, three men, one woman, and two children, were seized as hostages.

Cochise quickly rallied his warriors. That evening a wagon train entered Apache Pass. The Indians attacked, captured two Americans, and tied the eight Mexican teamsters to the wheels and burned them. The next morning Cochise and a large band of Chiricahua and Coyotero Apaches attacked the Butterfield station, taking another prisoner. Cochise then offered to trade Bascom his three American prisoners for the six Apache captives. Bascom refused. Then, realizing his tenuous position, the lieutenant sent couriers to Fort Buchanan for aid. On February 10, Lieutenant B. J. D. Irwin arrived with mounted infantrymen from Fort Buchanan and three Apache warriors captured en route. Four days later, Lieutenant Isaiah N. Moore reached the scene with seventy more soldiers from Fort Breckinridge, causing Cochise to lift his siege and flee into the mountains. The soldiers, as they scouted in the vicinity, found the bodies of the American hostages mutilated beyond individual recognition. Moore, the senior officer, ordered the six adult Apache males hanged to trees near the graves of the American victims.

The Bascom Affair so enraged Cochise that he launched a long and total war, one that cost hundreds of lives and thousands of dollars' worth of damage to property, for he intended nothing less than the total extermination of all Americans in Arizona. Bascom was commended by his superiors for his part in this episode. This incident occurred just as the Civil War was breaking out in the East. The effect of the war was quickly felt in Arizona, for the American soldiers were withdrawn to the Río Grande Valley to protect New Mexico from invading Texas Confederates. Charles D. Poston was forced to close the operations of his Sonora Exploring and Mining Company and flee the territory for his life. Only Sylvester Mowry tried to continue mining. He and loyal employees barricaded themselves at the Mowry Mine, but Mowry was forced to undergo the humiliation of seeing Cochise brazenly riding around out of rifle shot on Mowry's favorite horse. Tucson

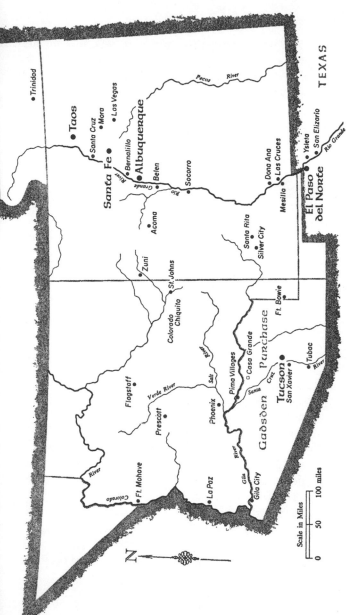

Arizona in the 1860's, showing also the outline of the Territory of New Mexico. *Drawn by Don Bufkin*

became a center of refuge for survivors, who moved there to avoid the fate of so many unprotected Arizonans— death at the hands of an aroused Apache nation. Not only were Apaches killing these Arizonans, but so also were Americans killing each other in that most tragic of all conflicts, civil war. The early 1860's were not pleasant years in the territory.

YANKEE AND REBEL IN THE DESERT

When angry Texans gathered in their secession convention in Austin in January, 1861, to shout through a vote of withdrawal from the Union, they were so certain that the Territory of New Mexico (which then included Arizona) would join the Southern cause that they appointed two commissioners to invite New Mexico to do so. Simeon Hart, one of the commissioners, allowed little time to lapse. On February 1, 1861, he wrote an inflammatory letter that was printed three weeks later in the *Mesilla Times*. In this letter he called on the residents of the Gadsden Purchase area (by which he actually meant Arizona, for southern New Mexico and southern Arizona of today then were called Arizona or Gadsdonia) to join with "those who have ever sympathized with you" against the "fanaticism of the North." In that same letter he urged that a secession convention be held at Mesilla on March 16. Hart's call for a secession convention was enthusiastically endorsed by prominent Arizonans. In 1860 the residents of the Gadsden strip had proclaimed a separate Territory of Arizona and had elected Dr. Lewis S. Owings their provisional governor. Owings supported the call for a convention, as did James A. Lucas and Granville H. Oury, also well known in Arizona. That convention was held on schedule in Mesilla with Lucas presiding.

The other commissioner from Texas, Philemon T. Herbert, addressed the convention, but it was his law partner, W. Claude Jones, who made the most rousing speech: "Has not [the North] treated us with cold and criminal neglect, and has this corrupt sectional [Republican] party taken any steps toward our organization? . . . The hell of abolitionism glooms to the north—the Eden of liberty, equality, and right smiles upon you from the south! Choose ye between them."

And choose they did—unanimously—to secede. In their resolution they repudiated the Republican party, severed ties with the Union, and asked to join the Confederacy. On March 23 a similar meeting occurred in Tucson. The presiding officer, Mark Aldrich, was the richest merchant in town and decidedly pro-Southern. Like the gathering at Mesilla, the Tucson convention denounced the North and asked the Confederacy to extend to Arizona "the protection necessary to the proper development and advancement of the Territory."

When news of the Southern victory at Fort Sumter reached Tucson in mid-May, a wild celebration occurred, during which a Confederate flag was presented to a volunteer company of "Arizona Rangers." An improvised military band played "Dixie's Land," and the crowd marched to Joshua Sledd's billiard saloon, where a flagpole was erected. The Confederate banner was raised aloft "with music, cheering, and speeches." The sentiment in Arizona was staunchly pro-Southern. Nor did Lieutenant Colonel, later General, Edward R. S. Canby help change this sentiment. Canby, senior Union officer in the District of New Mexico, decided to consolidate his remaining troops at the principal posts along the Río Grande. He therefore ordered army detachments in present Arizona to withdraw eastward, leaving Arizona without protection from the Apaches.

Confederates quickly took advantage of pro-Southern sentiment in Arizona. John Robert Baylor, who was newly commissioned a lieutenant colonel of the Texas Mounted Rifles, marched from San Antonio in June, 1861, and arrived at El Paso on July 1. Twenty-three days later, without specific authorization from his superiors, he moved into southern New Mexico toward Mesilla with the stated purpose of "protecting the citizens of Arizona." At nearby Fort Fillmore the Union commander, Major Isaac Lynde, first advanced toward the Confederates, then retreated northward up the Río Grande. Baylor followed, overtook Lynde at San Augustine Pass, twenty-two miles north of Mesilla, and captured the Union force without firing a shot. The *Mesilla Times* jubilantly headlined, "Arizona is Free AT LAST." On August 1, 1861, Baylor by proclamation took possession of the "Territory of Arizona" in the name of the Confederacy: "The social and political condition of Arizona being little short of general anarchy, and the people being literally destitute of law, order, and protection, the said Territory . . . is hereby declared temporarily organized as a military government, until such time as Congress may otherwise provide." He defined Confederate Arizona as all of the Territory of New Mexico south of the thirty-fourth parallel. Baylor immodestly named himself governor.

Baylor's actions met enthusiastic approval in the territory. At a subsequent meeting held in Tucson, Granville H. Oury was elected delegate to the Confederate Congress then meeting in Richmond. Oury traveled to the Confederate capital, and on November 22, 1861, John H. Reagan of Texas introduced a bill to recognize Arizona as a Confederate territory. That bill passed on January 13, 1862, and was signed by Jefferson Davis, to take effect on February 14, 1862 (exactly fifty years before Arizona statehood). This act stipulated the thirty-fourth parallel as the boundary but asserted the Confederate right to take the remainder of New Mexico. Slavery was to be protected, Oury was seated in the Confederate Congress, and President Davis confirmed Baylor as governor of the territory.

John Robert Baylor proved a tempestuous governor. When chided in the *Mesilla Times* for failure to do battle with General Canby, Baylor dueled with the editor, Robert P. Kelley, and killed him. He organized the Arizona Guards, a volunteer force organized to combat the Indians then terrorizing much of Arizona, and on March 20, 1862, issued his instructions to them: "You will . . . use all means to persuade the Apaches or any tribe to come in for the purpose of making peace, and when you get them together kill all the grown Indians and take the children prisoners and sell them to defray the expense of killing the Indians. Buy whiskey and such other goods as may be necessary for the Indians and I will order vouchers given to cover the amount expended. Leave nothing undone to insure success, and have a sufficient number of men around to allow no Indian to escape." Baylor was charged with ordering poisoned food left for Indian consumption and with inducing Indians to come in under flags of truce only to slaughter them.

While these events were transpiring, another Confederate force was preparing to invade New Mexico. Chosen by President Jefferson Davis for this purpose was Henry Hopkins Sibley. A major in the United States Army in 1861, Sibley had resigned his commission on May 13, 1861, bitter at his failure to be promoted beyond the rank of major. On July 8, he was commissioned a Confederate brigadier general, ordered to raise a brigade of cavalry in Texas, march the force to New Mexico, conquer the territory, and become its governor. His Army of New Mexico was recruited at San Antonio. Late in October and early in November, 1861, this army marched to the northwest, arriving at El Paso on December 14. There Sibley assumed command of all Confederate forces in West Texas, Arizona, and New Mexico. On December 20 he issued a proclamation to the people in which he listed the many benefits of Confederate rule and protection. And he invited one and all—Union soldiers as well as civilians—to join with him and the Southern cause. That same day he issued General Orders No. 12 which stated that his proclamation was "not . . . intended to abrogate or supersede the powers of Col. John R. Baylor, as civil and military governor of Arizona." However, all of Baylor's men were mustered into Sibley's Army of New Mexico.

On February 21, Sibley's force fought its first contest with Canby's troops, who were at Fort Craig, New Mexico, some sixty miles south of Albuquerque. During the morning hours it appeared that Canby's men would win the Battle of Valverde. Sibley, sensing defeat and quite drunk, later reported, "At 1:30 P.M., having become completely exhausted and finding myself no longer able to keep the saddle, I sent my aides and other staff officers to report to Colonel Green." Tom Green, the subordinate who assumed command, knew only one bit of strategy, a charge. This charge turned the tide of battle and caused New Mexican volunteer forces to break and retreat. Canby and his troops fell back within the walls of Fort Craig, expecting total defeat. About seven that evening, however, Sibley resumed command, and his first order was to break off the engagement. Then, leaving Canby and the Federals inside the fort, he marched his army up the Río Grande. Albuquerque and Santa Fe were taken with ease, leaving only Fort Union, a supply post in northeastern New Mexico, and Fort Craig in Federal hands. Sibley issued the usual proclamation, promising great improvements in New Mexico under Confederate auspices, but his undisciplined men began looting and turned most citizens against the invaders.

Meanwhile, one part of Sibley's Army of New Mexico was busy to the west. Before the Battle of Valverde, Sibley had sent about two hundred men to Tucson. Called "Arizona Volunteers," these men were commanded by Captain Sherrod Hunter. They arrived in Tucson on February 28 to be greeted enthusiastically by the population. Union sympathizers either remained silent, slipped away to California or Sonora, or else saw their property confiscated and themselves ordered out of town. Estevan Ochoa was such a man. He refused to take an oath of loyalty to the Confederacy, declaring that he owed everything he had to the United States. His property was taken, he was given only an hour to pack, and then was forced to ride alone out of town headed for Union lines. Owing to the ferocity of the Apaches, his loyalty to the United States seemed almost suicidal—but he managed to reach Canby's headquarters in New Mexico safely.

Hunter's troops did attempt to pacify the Apaches, and he perhaps hoped to capture Fort Yuma to the west and thereby encourage Southern sympathizers in California. One detachment of his men reached the Pima Indian villages on the Gila River. There they confiscated fifteen hundred sacks of wheat from Indian trader A. M. White; the wheat was returned to the Pimas, and Hunter was notified that it had been purchased to feed a Union force of California Volunteers marching eastward under the command of Colonel James Henry Carleton. A down-Easter from Maine, Carleton had eighteen hundred men at Fort Yuma. Knowing that the Confederates were at Tucson, Carleton sent Captain William McCleave with a scouting party to reconnoiter. McCleave arrived at the Pima villages only to be captured by the Confederates and marched eastward to a Southern prison. Carleton thereupon ordered Lieutenant Colonel J. R. West ahead with men to open the road to Tucson. At the Pima villages the Federals learned from the Pima Indians of a Confederate detachment near Picacho Pass, and Lieutenant James Barrett was sent with a dozen troops to capture the rebels. A battle occurred between the two forces on April 15, 1862—the Battle of Picacho Pass, sometimes called the westernmost battle of the Civil War—with the Confederates killing Lieutenant Barrett and two enlisted men, losing two men themselves. The skirmish amounted to a Confederate victory, but it availed them little. Captain Hunter realized he could not stand against eighteen hundred California Volunteers. He ordered a retreat, for he had learned on May 4 that Sibley's Army of New Mexico had suffered a sharp reversal.

In New Mexico Sibley had determined upon the conquest of Fort Union. He sent approximately one thousand men under the command of Colonel William Scurry to accomplish this task. At Glorieta Pass on March 26–28, the Texans met Federal troops reinforced by Colorado Volunteers and won the battle. During the conflict, however, the Confederate supply wagons were captured, and Scurry had to order a retreat. Faced with Colorado Volunteers coming from the north, a Union army marching

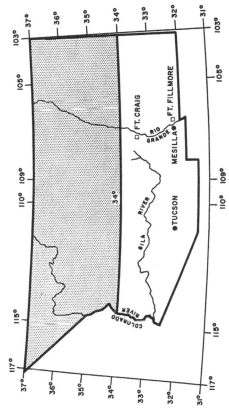

The Territory of Arizona as proclaimed by the Confederates and by General Carleton. *Drawn by Don Bufkin*

southwest from Missouri, and Canby's troops to the south, Sibley determined to retreat to Texas. By April, 1862, Confederate New Mexico had ceased to exist. Sherrod Hunter likewise retreated toward Texas, as did Baylor from Mesilla—and Confederate Arizona was no more.

Meanwhile, Colonel Carleton was marching eastward from Fort Yuma. Colonel West's advance detachment arrived in Tucson in May. These troops established Camp Tucson at the site of the present Santa Rita Hotel (in 1873 the post was moved nine miles east and designated Fort Lowell). These men were followed in June by the remainder of the California Column. Carleton and his fifteen hundred men marched through heat and choking dust, drinking foul water and eating bad food, sweating and swearing. They arrived in Tucson early in June, and there on the eighth Carleton issued his proclamation: "In the present chaotic state in which Arizona is to be found: with no civil officers to administer the laws: indeed with an utter absence of all civil authority: and with no security of life or property within its borders: it becomes the duty of the undersigned to represent the authority of the United States over the people of Arizona." He insisted that all residents swear allegiance to the United States, that they have a lawful occupation, and that no subversive words or deeds be tolerated. He did tax the merchants of Tucson for war expenses, with an extremely heavy tax on gamblers and saloon-keepers which was to be used to care for his sick and wounded soldiers. And he arrested a number of political prisoners, chief among whom was Sylvester Mowry, accused of treasonable complicity with the rebels. Mowry was sent to prison in Fort Yuma and his mine confiscated. In November, 1862, Mowry was released unconditionally, but his mine had been stripped of most of its value in the interim. Later it was sold at auction. In December, 1863, Mowry sued Carleton in a California court for one million dollars in damages but received nothing from the suit.

With Arizona secured to the Union cause, Carleton prepared to link up with Canby in New Mexico. On July 4, 1862, Captain Thomas Roberts with 126 men, twenty-two wagons, and two howitzers left Tucson for New Mexico following the Butterfield stage route. At Apache Pass on July 15, this column was attacked by 700 Apaches under Cochise. A ten-hour battle followed. Only the howitzers prevented a massacre of the troops. The next day Roberts was able to force his way through the pass. American losses were two killed, while 63 Indians died. It was the largest battle between Americans and Apaches in Arizona's history.

Carleton, now a brigadier general, left Tucson on July 20 with fourteen hundred troops. A week later he was at Apache Pass where he paused to order a fort constructed. Named Fort Bowie, it commanded the pass, as well as the spring which provided the best water supply for miles, and offered protection to travelers and wagon trains in the following years. Carleton reached Fort Thorn, New Mexico, on August 7, and immediately began ordering patrols southward toward El Paso. In the months ahead his men would reach into West Texas, probing for rebels.

Carleton's Territory of Arizona, which, like Baylor's, included all of present New Mexico and Arizona south of the thirty-fourth parallel, proved troublesome for him to administer; but he ruled with a heavy hand, earning the nickname "Mogul." His greatest problem was not Southern sympathizers—these he arrested—but the Indians. As he had few regular troops available, he raised companies of volunteers. On October 12, 1862, he issued orders for fighting the Mescalero Apaches and the Navahos. Kit Carson, the former mountain man and army scout, was commissioned a colonel of volunteers and sent to fight these Indians. His orders were, "All Indian men of that tribe are to be killed whenever and wherever you find them; the women and children will not be harmed, but you will take them prisoners." Carson was instructed not to make peace but to kill.

In the summer of 1863, Carson gathered 736 men and actively pushed war against the Navahos into their traditional strongholds in northeastern Arizona and northwestern New Mexico. By September his attacks proved so effective that the Navahos began surrendering in large numbers. Carleton had the prisoners placed on the Bosque Redondo, a reservation he established in eastern New Mexico on the Pecos River for them and for the Mescalero Apaches. Still Carson persisted in his campaign against the Navahos until, by January, 1864, the only members of that tribe still at large were in Canyon de Chelly. Carson systematically pushed into what he called "the celebrated Gibraltar of the Navahos." Where American bullets failed, cold and hunger succeeded, and the last hostiles surrendered. By April of 1864 more than eight thousand Navahos were under secure American control, all to be located at Bosque Redondo. That location proved a disaster to the Navahos. Many of them died in a climate far different from their traditional homeland, others ran away, and quarreling with the Mescaleros was constant. In June, 1868, the government agreed to their return to a reservation created especially for them in northwestern New Mexico and northeastern Arizona, with headquarters at Fort Wingate, New Mexico.

While Carson was achieving his noteworthy success in subduing the Navahos, other military men and volunteers were contending with the Apaches. In early 1863 Colonel J. R. West was assigned the task of defeating the Mimbreño Apaches, who frequented the headwaters of the Gila River. During this campaign, Mangas Coloradas was captured, reportedly by trickery. Then, according to West's report, Mangas was killed while rushing his guards. A witness, Daniel E. Conner, later wrote that Colonel West had told the guards, "Men, that old murderer has got away from every soldier command and has left a trail of blood for five hundred miles on the old stage line. I want him dead or alive tomorrow morning, do you understand. *I want him dead.*" The next morning Mangas was dead. His death caused the Mimbreños to accept reservations or to flee to the west and join forces with Cochise and the Chiricahua Apaches. Carleton's plans for other Apache groups did not progress so well, however. The Chiricahuas were not subdued, nor were the Apache groups in central Arizona contained. But in the northern part of the territory some success was achieved because of the influx of miners.

General Carleton apparently had some hopes of getting rich from mining. Joseph Reddeford Walker was in New Mexico in 1862 when Carleton arrived, and the two men seem to have entered into some kind of partnership agreement. With Carleton's permission Walker entered Arizona, journeyed to Tucson, and went north. On the Hassayampa (five miles from the present Prescott) Walker's party made a strike. More prospectors rushed to the region, and other discoveries were made in what came to be known as the Walker Mining District. For the protection of these miners, Carleton on October 23, 1863, created the District of Northern Arizona and ordered Fort Whipple established.

Civilians likewise fought the Indians, noteworthy among them King S. Woolsey. A resident of the territory since 1860, Woolsey had joined the Confederacy but was prevented from active service by illness. Next he established a ranch east of Prescott on the Agua Fria, where he made a living selling hay to the army. On several occasions he organized Indian-fighting expeditions with civilian volunteers. In January, 1864, after raids had become too frequent, he gathered thirty Americans and fourteen Indian allies and marched in pursuit of Apaches. In the vicinity of Fish Creek Canyon he came upon Apaches. The Apaches agreed to a council at which, on Woolsey's signal, the Americans opened fire, killing many Apaches and teaching the others to distrust Americans. This incident was labeled the "Massacre at Bloody Tanks." According to some stories, Woolsey also gave pinole (a mixture of ground corn and sugar) loaded with strychnine to the Indians, thereby killing many of them.

Arizona therefore gained a measure of peace during the Civil War. The Indian problem had not been solved, but more protection was available than at any previous time. Tucson almost doubled in size between 1862, when Carleton arrived, and 1865, when the Civil War ended. Troops stationed at Tubac enabled the Sonora Exploring and Mining Company, now owned in large measure by Samuel Colt, the gunmaker, to reopen the Heintzelman Mine. Army posts, needing grain, hay, and food supplies, brought a measure of economic prosperity to the territory. But Arizona's greatest gain from the Civil War was separate territorial status.

BE IT ENACTED: THE CREATION OF THE TERRITORY

By 1862 no less than three territories of Arizona had been proclaimed: that by Arizonans themselves in 1860, with Dr. Lewis S. Owings as governor; that by the Confederate Congress in 1862, with Colonel John Robert Baylor as governor; and that by General James H. Carleton in 1862, with himself as chief executive. All were similar in that they called for a division of the old Territory of New Mexico along the thirty-fourth parallel (the Gadsden Purchase area). And all three proved abortive efforts to separate Arizona from New Mexico: the effort in 1860 by Arizonans was never recognized by anyone; the Confederate territory died with the abandonment of the region by rebel troops; and Carleton's proclamation never received sanction in Washington.

Less than a month after the Confederate Territory of Arizona became official on February 14, 1862, James M. Ashley, a Republican congressman from Ohio, introduced a bill in the House to organize Arizona as a territory of the United States. This bill, designated H. R. 357, stipulated that the new territory would be separated from New Mexico by a north-south line at approximately 109 degrees west longitude, although that meridian was not specifically mentioned. Rather, it said that Arizona would comprise "all that part of the present Territory of New Mexico situated west of a line running due south from the point where the southwest corner of the Territory of Colorado joins the northern boundary of the Territory of New Mexico." It was no surprise that Ashley of Ohio introduced this bill. Much of the office work of the Sonora Exploring and Mining Company was performed in Cincinnati, many of the stockholders in the company were residents of Ohio, and federal organization of a Territory of Arizona would bring protection from Indians to mining ventures in the region. Ohioans stood to profit from the creation of a federal Territory of Arizona. Congressmen and senators from the state realized this, and they led the fight to win passage for Ashley's bill.

As Ashley was chairman of the House Committee on Territories, his bill received a respectful hearing. Charles A. Wickliffe, a former governor of Missouri and onetime postmaster general, stated a major point of opposition on March 24. He said even if Arizona became a territory, no federal officials could go there because Arizona had been occupied by Confederate troops. Ashley answered that such was not the case (although, in truth, Sherrod Hunter was in Tucson with his Arizona Volunteers and would be until late April). Then, on May 8, William A. Wheeler, a Republican from New York, stated, "So far as the records of the House throw any light upon the subject, no single inhabitant within its proposed bounds has asked for this organization." Wickliffe rose to add that Apaches had driven every American settler from the territory and that Congress would be hard-pressed to organize a territory without settlers. Wheeler continued the attack, stating that Arizona was "the home not of those seeking to make farms and build school houses, but of the adventurous miner who seeks sudden wealth . . . to be enjoyed elsewhere." Finally, Wheeler asserted, "There are not now one thousand whites in the whole of Arizona. We are asked to incur . . . an expenditure [of] at least $50,000. . . . Sir, a territorial government at fifty dollars per head . . . is an expense which the people of this country are just now not in a mood to indulge."

First territorial officials of Arizona: seated (left to right),
Joseph P. Allyn, Governor John N. Goodwin, and Richard
C. McCormick; standing (left to right), Henry W. Fleury,
Milton B. Duffield, and Almon Gage. *Arizona Pioneers'
Historical Society*

The steamer *Gila* on the Colorado River. *Arizona Pioneers'*

A train arrives at Benson in the 1890's. *Arizona Pioneers' Historical Society*

Pipe Springs National Monument. *National Park Service*

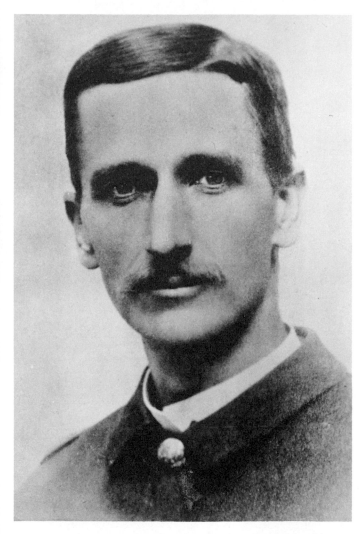

Lieutenant Charles B. Gatewood, the man who induced
Geronimo to surrender. *Arizona Pioneers' Historical Society*

"El Potrero," the home of Pete Kitchen. *National Park Service*

Contemporary view of the Sierra Bonita Ranch of Henry Clay Hooker. *National Park Service*

Logging by the Arizona Lumber Company near Flagstaff in the 1890's. *Arizona Pioneers' Historical Society*

John S. Watts, territorial delegate from New Mexico, joined Ashley in pushing the bill. He stated that he had introduced one bill to create a Territory of Arizona, and that residents of Arizona "had petitioned and prayed and asked and knocked at the doors of Congress" for separate territorial status. He said that the census of 1860 had listed 6,462 whites, 4,040 Indians, and 21 free Negroes in Arizona —a total of 10,523 inhabitants. But, he asserted, these figures were of no consequence, for if "but one solitary white man" was there, he was entitled to civil law and protection of life and property. "We have not a single fort, a single soldier, or a single man with which to enforce our treaty stipulations," he declared, referring to the clause in the Treaty of Guadalupe Hidalgo which extended to people in Arizona all "the privileges and immunities" of citizens of the United States. "Is there any fair and candid man, any just man," thundered Watts, "who can for a moment pretend that it is not a serious and solemn duty to extend protection to that country?"

John Addison Gurley, another congressman from Ohio, declared that $1,000,000 had been spent to open the gold and silver mines of Arizona; was not the government bound by honor, he asked, to protect those who had gone there and who had invested there? Watts then presented an argument better calculated to impress the congressmen than any that had been presented before. In his hand he held aloft a specimen of silver ore, a choice sample from the Heintzelman Mine (provided conveniently by Charles D. Poston, who was in Washington lobbying passage of H. R. 357). The California mines, asserted Watts, had increased the national currency by $75,000,000; Arizona stood ready to do the same if only the government extended organization and protection from the Indians.

Then, feeling that Arizona's charms were not sufficiently known by his colleagues, Watts attempted a description: "An Italian sunset never threw its gentle rays over more lovely valleys or heaven-kissing hills, valleys harmonious with the music of a thousand sparkling rills, mountains shining with untold millions of mineral wealth, wooing the hand of capital and labor to possess and use it." He continued, "The virgin rays of the morning sun first kiss the brow of its lofty mountains, and the parting beams of the setting sun linger fondly around their sublime summits, unwilling to leave to darkness and to night such beauty and such grandeur." In a final appeal, couched in all the grandiloquent oratory of which he was capable, Watts concluded, "Let it not be said of us that, while we are ready to spend untold millions of money and thousands of lives to protect our own lives and property, the appeal of this distant people falls upon our bosoms 'Cold as moonbeams on the barren heath.' Let it not be said of us that we have the power to conquer and annex provinces, but not to protect and defend them."

The crucial vote came on May 8, 1862, after further arguments by Ashley. H. R. 357 passed the House by a vote of seventy-two to fifty-two. Then the bill went to the Senate. Lyman Trumbull of Illinois spearheaded the opposition, using many of the same arguments that had been heard in the House: Arizona had too few people, that protection would best come by sending more troops, not by creating a separate territory. On July 3 he said he had learned there were 6,482 residents in the proposed territory, but that this number was insufficient to justify creating a territory.

Benjamin Franklin Wade, a former Whig turned Republican from Ohio, championed the measure. His position as chairman of the Senate Committee on Territories lent weight to his support. In his speech he dismissed Trumbull's arguments as trifling, declaring that Arizona was rich in minerals, rich in agricultural potential, and rich in prospects. Despite Wade's favorable comments and those of others, a vote to table the measure carried twenty-five to thirteen—and thus it was not placed on the Senate's calendar again until February 19, 1863. During this interim men like Poston and Samuel P. Heintzelman, now a major general of volunteers, lobbied quite effectively to win support for the bill.

When the measure came up for consideration in early 1863, Senator Trumbull again led the opposition. Wade on February 20 thundered his opinion at his colleagues: "The richest country in the world, we are told, should not be organized so that the American people can feel safe, and be under the protection of the law when they go there. The Senator [Trumbull] thinks, because we have a civil war on our hands, we ought to give up everything. . . . Are we to be told that we must not organize our Territories, that we must not develop our wealth because we are involved in civil war?"

Opposition to H. R. 357 declined at this point. Trumbull's motion to postpone further consideration of the bill was defeated on February 20. That same day, without delay, the Senate passed the bill by a vote of twenty-five to twelve. Two Democrats joined twenty-three Republicans in favor of it, while six Republicans, four Democrats, and two "old-line" Whigs stood against it. Four days later, on February 24, 1863, President Abraham Lincoln signed the statute. Charles D. Poston was in Lincoln's office for the event. At that time he presented to Lincoln an inkstand, fashioned by Tiffany's of New York City, which was used for the signing; the President's name was engraved on one side of the inkstand, Poston's on the other side. The silver used to make this inkstand came from the Heintzelman Mine in Arizona—appropriately so, for Arizona's mineral wealth had done more than any man to carry the bill through Congress.

In April, 1884, Poston wrote an article entitled "Scraps of History Furnished by One Who Helped to Make the Scraps," which appeared in the Tucson *Citizen*. In this article, which supposedly told how Arizona had achieved territorial status, Poston declared that he had been in Washington in December, 1862, lobbying in behalf of Arizona. He asserted that, on the advice of Senator Wade and Congressman Gurley, he had organized an oyster supper for lame-duck congressmen "defeated in their own districts for the next term, who wanted to go west and offer their political services to the 'galoots.'" At this supper, according to Poston, a slate of territorial officials was arranged. "But towards the last it occurred to my obfusticated [*sic*] brain that my name did not appear on the slate, and in the language of Daniel Webster, I exclaimed, 'Gentlemen, what is to become of me?' Gourley replied, 'O! We will make you Indian agent.' So the bill passed and Lincoln signed all the commissions, and the oyster supper was paid for and we were all happy, and Arizona was launched on the political sea under command of as 'Mild mannered men/ As ever cut a throat or scuttled a ship.'"

Poston's story, while colorful, contains little truth. Five of the officials first appointed to offices in Arizona were not members of Congress. His time sequence was incorrect, for in December, 1862 (when the incident supposedly occurred), H. R. 357 had already passed the House. Other inconsistencies also are contained in the account. Poston did have an impish sense of humor, and he was prone to exaggerate his own importance—thereby earning for himself the nickname "Father of Arizona."

On March 4, 1863, Lincoln named his appointees to the new territory. John A. Gurley was to be governor, but Gurley died on August 18 that year, never having left Washington, and John Noble Goodwin of Maine, who had been named chief justice of the Territorial Supreme Court in March, became Gurley's replacement. Other officials included Richard C. McCormick, secretary; William F. Turner, chief justice, replacing Goodwin; William T. Howell and Joseph P. Allyn, associate justices; Almon Gage, district attorney; Milton B. Duffield, United States marshal; and Poston, superintendent of Indian affairs.

These men made their way to Arizona in two parties. Poston and several minor officials went overland to San Francisco and then made their way to Arizona. Goodwin, a lawyer from Maine who had served one term in Congress, went overland in company with McCormick and Allyn to Cincinnati. There they were joined by Howell, Gage, and others so that their party numbered eighteen. The officials and an escort of soldiers went west by way of Fort Leavenworth, Fort Riley, and the Santa Fe Trail. In New Mexico they conferred with General Carleton, who suggested the site of the capital should be in northern Arizona near the mineral discoveries of the Walker Mining District (in which Carleton had a stake). Goodwin and the other territorial officials agreed to this suggestion. Therefore they went directly west from Albuquerque instead of toward Tucson, their original goal. On this route, in the dead of winter, they arrived in Arizona—and separate territorial government became a reality at last.

THE FOUNDING FATHERS

Probably it was December 27, 1863, when Governor Goodwin and his party crossed 109° 2′ 59.25″ west longitude—and thus entered Arizona. They were not certain that they were in Arizona, however, and thus traveled two more days before pausing to enact a ceremony of formally proclaiming the territory's existence in fact. On December 29 at Navajo Springs in a raging snowstorm, the civilians and soldiers held their formal ceremony. The Reverend Hiram Walker Reed offered a prayer, then each official took his oath of office. Richard C. McCormick, secretary of the territory, made a speech in which he declared, "After a long and trying journey, we have arrived within the limits of Arizona. These broad plains and hills form a part of the district over which, as representatives of the United States, we are to establish a civil government." Alluding to the recent Confederate invasion, he said, "Happily, although claimed by those now in hostility to the Federal arms, we take possession of the Territory without resort to military force." Then, perhaps thinking of the many Southern sympathizers in the territory, he concluded, "The flag which I hoist in token of our authority is no new and untried banner. For nearly a century it has been the recognized, the honored, the loved emblem of law and liberty."

After McCormick's speech came the governor's proclamation, read both in English and in Spanish, "I, JOHN N. GOODWIN, having been appointed by the President of the United States, and duly qualified, as Governor of the TERRITORY OF ARIZONA, do hereby announce that by virtue of the powers with which I am invested by an Act of Congress of the United States, providing a temporary government for the Territory, I shall this day proceed to organize said government." The capital, according to this proclamation, was to be "for the present at or near Ft. Whipple." Goodwin's proclamation, when circulated, also called for the taking of a census, dividing the territory into judicial districts, and the election of a legislative assembly.

Goodwin and the territorial party arrived at Fort Whipple on January 22, 1864. At this time the post was located in the Chino Valley near the mines originally discovered in the Walker Mining District; however, the center of mining activities had moved about twenty miles southeast of the fort. Therefore in April a new townsite was selected nearer to the mines. The little town that grew there first was called Goodwin in honor of the governor. Another name suggested for it was Granite, for it was located on Granite Creek. Secretary McCormick, the ambitious and lettered secretary, proffered the final designation: Prescott. He had read William Hickling Prescott's classic *History of the Conquest of Mexico* and noted the proximity of Arizona to Mexico. It was his idea that the capital be named in honor of a great historian of the neighbor to the south. The townsite was surveyed by Governor Goodwin, marked off, and dedicated on May 30. Looking to the future, Governor Goodwin insisted that the streets be one hundred feet wide. The first sale of lots brought $3,927.50, with an entire square block atop the highest point in the townsite reserved for public buildings.

Homes were erected quickly. Most were of log construction, and in architectural form were typically Yankee. One of the first business establishments opened was a newspaper. Secretary McCormick had brought a portable printing press with him, and he began publishing the *Arizona*

Miner, the first newspaper printed north of the Gila River. A billiard saloon, two doctors' offices, stores, a restaurant, and the Jackson Hotel completed the creation of the city. Fort Whipple was moved to a site near the new city, and it likewise was of log construction—but was not imposing. A contemporary description called it "a ramshackle tumble-down palisade of unbarked pine logs, hewn from the adjacent slopes. Quarters for both officers and men were of logs with the exception of a one-room shanty on the apex of the hill nearest town, built of unseasoned, unpainted pine planks." The governor's mansion was the most imposing structure in town. Costing $6,000 and built of logs, it differed from other buildings in that it was two stories high.

Governor Goodwin decided shortly to make a tour of the territory to gain firsthand information. He started at the mining camps in the vicinity and went east as far as the Verde and Salinas rivers; in April and May, he went south to Tucson and west to Yuma. He incorporated the municipality of Tucson at the request of its residents on May 11, appointing William S. Oury mayor and Mark Aldrich, among others, to the city council. This was a smart political move on his part, for both Oury and Aldrich had been well-known Confederate sympathizers. While Goodwin was touring, Marshal Duffield was taking the census. As place of birth, according to this census, Arizonans listed every state in the Union, along with many foreign countries—Mexico, not unexpectedly, leading in this category. The major occupations were mining, farming, and soldiering. The census also called for an estimation of wealth. These estimates ranged from a high of $52,000, reported by Mark Aldrich, to 25 cents, reported by Thomas J. Goodman. The total population was 4,573.

On the basis of this census, Goodwin on May 26 called for an election of territorial officials. This election, held on July 18, saw nine council members and eighteen legislators chosen. The most hotly contested office was territorial delegate to Congress, which was won by Charles D. Poston with 514 votes, more than the combined total of his three opponents. The First Territorial Legislature then convened in Prescott on September 26. It had to meet in Governor Goodwin's home, for the capital was not yet completed. That legislature created a board of regents for a proposed university, divided Arizona into four counties (Mohave, Yavapai, Yuma, and Pima), incorporated several road companies and chartered several railroads, and appropriated $1,500 for public education. The greatest accomplishment of this legislature was the approval of a code of laws compiled by Associate Justice William T. Howell and named in his honor: the Howell Code. What this legislative session could not agree on, however, was the permanent location of the capital. Prescott was far from the settled areas, and many Arizonans objected to the location, but Governor Goodwin wanted it in Prescott, and he had his way.

Goodwin did not meet with the Second Territorial Legislature, although he was still the official governor. In the regular election in September, 1865, he had run for the office of territorial delegate to Congress and had won, defeating Poston and Associate Justice Allyn. Thus in December, when the Second Legislature convened, Goodwin was in Washington, simultaneously holding two offices and drawing two salaries. Acting as governor in his absence was Secretary Richard C. McCormick. Called "Slippery Dick" or "Little Mac," McCormick was a New Yorker by birth, a journalist by profession. He had served as a war correspondent in both the Crimean War and the Civil War and then had held the position of chief clerk in the Department of Agriculture. As acting governor, and as governor in his own right after April 10, 1866, he was active in promoting education, mining, agriculture, roads, and railroads. McCormick also pushed war on the marauding Apaches, and he suggested that the federal government should purchase sufficient land from Mexico to give Arizona a port on the Gulf of California. Finally, at his behest, the capital was moved from Prescott to Tucson in 1867. McCormick's popularity in Arizona was shown by his election, in the fall of 1868, to the most coveted post the territory could bestow, delegate to Congress, to which he was re-elected in 1870 and 1872. In Washington he proved very active in Arizona's behalf, especially as a publicist who wrote extensively extolling the virtues of the territory.

The next chief executive of Arizona was Anson Peaceley-Killen Safford, a Vermonter who had worked in the gold fields in California and Nevada. In 1867 he had been named surveyor general of Nevada, a post he held until April 7, 1869, when President Ulysses Grant named him governor of Arizona. After a study of conditions in the territory, "Little Saff" asked for arms and supplies from the army for use by companies of civilian volunteers. His first legislative session came in 1871, the Sixth Legislature (for after 1868 the legislature met only every two years). To this legislature Safford stressed the need of free public education. The legislators responded by creating a public school system, thus bestowing on Safford the title "Father of Arizona schools." That same legislature also created Maricopa County and dissolved Pah-Ute County. Pah-Ute County, established by the legislature in 1865, had comprised the present southern part of Nevada. Since Congress had taken this area from Arizona in 1866 and given it to Nevada, the legislature in 1871 simply was recognizing an accomplished fact. In the next several sessions of the legislature, Safford continued to push public education, agriculture, good roads, and confinement of the Indians on reservations. He invested heavily in mining ventures, the most successful one at Tombstone, which made him rich enough to retire to Florida.

Safford was succeeded by John Philo Hoyt in 1877. Hoyt, appointed by President Rutherford B. Hayes, was a native of Ohio, a Union Army veteran, a lawyer, and had served as secretary of Arizona Territory under Safford. His tenure, while brief, was a period of discoveries of rich mines, explorations for minerals, and general development of the territory. Still unsolved was the Apache problem, a problem that would haunt the next several administrations before a final solution was achieved. Hoyt served only until June 12, 1878, when he was asked to resign to make way for a political hack in need of a job. He was appointed to the Supreme Court in Washington Territory and became quite prominent there.

John Charles Frémont, the aging "Great Pathfinder," approached the Hayes administration in 1878 to ask for an appointment. President Hayes complied, feeling that the Republican party owed Frémont a debt. In 1864, when Lincoln had run for re-election on a Union ticket and some disgruntled Republicans had approached Frémont about running on a Republican ticket, Frémont had declined. Therefore, thought Hayes, the Republicans owed Frémont something for preventing a party split. Governor Hoyt was asked to resign, and in 1878, Frémont became governor of Arizona Territory. Frémont arrived in

Prescott, which had become the capital again in 1877, and met the Tenth Legislature in January, 1879. That legislature changed the surnames of eight people, divorced seventeen couples, created Apache County, and licensed gambling. It also authorized a lottery, which failed after federal postal officials refused to carry its advertisements. Frémont, however, was not really interested in what the legislature did. He used his time to invest in mining ventures, and he spent more time outside the territory than in it, traveling to New York and Washington several times at territorial expense. Once while in the East, Frémont suggested in an interview that water from the Colorado River be diverted to the Imperial Desert of southern California to form an inland sea for agricultural purposes. In Arizona, this idea was widely protested as pro-California and anti-Arizona.

Frémont also met the Eleventh Legislature (1881), which created Gila, Cochise, and Graham counties, repealed the lottery, and authorized the incorporation of the cities of Tombstone, Phoenix, and Prescott. Continued protests at Frémont's frequent absences from the territory finally led to his resignation on October 11, 1881. The New York *Herald* on October 25 commented that President Chester A. Arthur had requested the resignation and stated that Frémont "seemed to regard the climate and society of New York as more agreeable and attractive than that of Arizona." Even his mining investments had proved ill advised, for he did not profit from them as he had expected.

Next to govern Arizona was Frederick A. Tritle, who was appointed by President Arthur on February 6, 1882. Tritle is generally regarded as the first Arizonan to serve as territorial chief executive, although he had been there only slightly more than a year when appointed. A Pennsylvanian, lawyer, and businessman, he had arrived in Arizona in 1880, where he operated the United Verde Copper Company. Able and hard-working, Tritle enthusiastically promoted the interests of the territory. During his administration, the chief legislative accomplishment came in 1885 when the so-called "Thieving Thirteenth" created the University of Arizona and a normal college that would become Arizona State University. Tritle served as governor until October, 1885, when he resigned at the request of the Democratic administration of President Grover Cleveland. Afterward, Tritle remained in Arizona in business, as recorder of Yavapai County from 1894 to 1897, and was supervisor of the census in 1900 for the territory.

The first Democratic appointee to govern Arizona was Conrad Meyer Zulick, another Pennsylvanian. A lawyer, he had moved to the territory in 1883, settling at Tombstone. In 1885 he was retained by William Green's land and cattle company to perform some legal chores in Cananea, Sonora. There he was jailed because of disputed debts, and a United States marshal had to rescue him in a dramatic jailbreak so that he could assume his position as chief executive of Arizona. Zulick's three and one-half years as governor were stormy, for he held the notion that Indians were human beings and should be treated as such. He also was the governor who in 1889 signed the bill moving the capital to Phoenix, where it has since remained. He resigned in April, 1889, because of the return of a Republican administration at the national level. After leaving the governorship, he served in the Territorial Council (the upper house of the legislature) and ranched in Maricopa County.

Lewis Wolfley was a Pennsylvanian, as were his two predecessors, but he was reared in the border country between Ohio and Kentucky. A bachelor, he moved to Arizona in the early 1880's, living first at Tucson and then at Prescott, working as an engineer and promoter. Immediately after becoming governor in April, 1889, he became involved in numerous squabbles. Although a man of considerable talent and abilities, Wolfley was not a politician, found it difficult to compromise, and quarreled with elected officials. After a year and a half in office, he was removed by President Benjamin Harrison, to whom many complaints had been directed. He remained in Arizona, operating the Climax Mines on the Hassayampa.

Thus by 1890 certain trends were apparent in Arizona politics. Early governors had been political "carpetbaggers"—appointed officials from outside the territory who neither knew nor cared about Arizona's needs. By the end of this period the governors appointed were residents of Arizona. Also, by 1890 the complaints of Arizona's citizens were heeded in Washington, and unwanted governors were removed. The era of political carpetbagging had come to an end. With only a single exception, during Grover Cleveland's first administration, all the appointees were Republicans, as were lesser officials within the territory. Some of these individuals had performed outstanding service to Arizona, while some had been of poor caliber, but politically the territory was maturing. The founding days were over. And just as it was maturing politically, so also it was maturing in other areas of endeavor.

THE INDIAN WARS

Arizona at the end of the Civil War was still largely the Indian's domain. A few scattered villages—Tucson, Tubac, Prescott, Yuma—were lonely outposts of American settlement, islands of safety in a sea of murder and pillage. Kit Carson's winter campaign of 1863–64 had subdued the Navahos; reservations had been established for the Pimas, Maricopas, Papagos, and the Yumas; but the many subtribes of Apaches and the Yavapais had not been subdued or even appreciably contained. Both these groups for centuries had lived by raiding. Their economy, their social system, and their political structure were based in large measure on booty taken on the warpath. Hereditary chieftains in theory governed these tribes, but war chiefs rose to positions of prominence and power through their reputations as thieves and warriors. An Indian's wealth was measured by the number of horses and mules he owned, and these were usually acquired on raids. Indeed, raiding had been their way of life long before the arrival of the Spaniards, and such was their way of life after the coming of the Americans.

To the encroaching Americans, however, this system was contrary to law. These frontiersmen thought they owned Arizona by right of conquest, that the Indian was an impediment to "civilization," something to be removed as soon as possible. The white was a threat to the Indian, both physically and psychologically. Conflict between the two groups was inevitable. They fought, both sides losing something in the inevitable warfare.

Soon after his arrival, Governor Goodwin sought to organize a company of "Arizona Volunteers"—civilians who would bring peace to the land by force. These men were enlisted for a year, but before they could be organized changes occurred. On January 20, 1865, Arizona was separated from the Department of New Mexico and placed under the military Department of California. Exactly a month later Captain John S. Mason was appointed to command the District of Arizona. He arrived in June that year. First came a tour of inspection, after which he reported: "At the time of my arrival in the district, I believe every ranch had been deserted south of the Gila. The town of Tubac was entirely deserted, and the town of Tucson had about two hundred souls. North of the Gila, the roads were completely blockaded; the ranches, with one or two exceptions, abandoned, and most of the settlements were threatened with abandonment or annihilation."

Mason spread his few men among the existing posts and created several new ones. These posts included Camp Bowie, at Apache Pass; Fort Lowell, at Tucson; Camp Crittenden, at the site of old Fort Buchanan in southern Arizona; Camp Grant, at old Fort Breckinridge; Fort Goodwin, on the Gila; Fort McDowell, on the Río Verde in central Arizona; Fort Whipple, near Prescott; Camp Date Creek, thirty miles southwest of Prescott; and Camp Lincoln, on the upper Verde River. Mason used much of his manpower to construct roads, actually little more than paths, between these posts. Arizonans were unhappy with Mason's results, for they were scant. Citizens of the territory did not realize how little aid Mason was receiving from his superiors—who in turn had little aid to extend him. Congress in 1866 had cut the army back to 54,302 men and had determined that all Civil War surplus materials had to be used before new weapons and equipment were ordered. Reconstruction in the South occupied the attention of most of these troops, and few could be spared for frontier warfare.

Lieutenant Colonel Thomas C. Devon took command of the District of Arizona early in 1868 and vigorously pushed war against the hostiles. He also increased the number of army encampments within the territory to

Major army posts during the era of the Indian wars.
Drawn by Don Bufkin

eighteen. Still he accomplished few positive results. For example, between July, 1868, and June, 1869, more than fifty people were killed by the Apaches in Pima County alone. Arizonans protested to Washington, but to little avail. In the nation's capital, critics of Indian warfare had the ear of the Grant administration. These self-styled experts declared that the Indian would best respond to training in agrarian methods; that to this end the natives should be gathered on reservations where civilians, not army officers, would control their destiny; and that such civilian Indian agents should be nominated by various religious denominations. The result was Grant's Peace Policy—which meant that the eastern experts were to have their way. For Arizona this meant that reservation agents would be nominated by the Dutch Reformed church, and it meant frustration for the army.

In line with Grant's Peace Policy, Arizona on April 15, 1870, was separated from the Department of California to become a department itself. In command since 1869 was General George Stoneman, a cavalry officer who first had seen the territory as a member of Philip St. George Cooke's command during the Mexican War. Stoneman, following orders from Washington, attempted to persuade the Apaches to live peacefully on the reservations where they would be fed until they could be taught agricultural pursuits. Arizonans were enraged at this practice, for they believed such reservations to be nothing more than feeding stations for Apaches who slipped away regularly to kill and loot. They wanted no peace offensive; they wanted action. Out of this rage came the infamous Camp Grant Massacre.

In February, 1871, some three hundred Aravaipa Apaches, led by their chief Eskiminzin, surrendered to the commanding officer at Camp Grant, Lieutenant Royal E. Whitman. Placed in Aravaipa Canyon near the San Pedro River, these Indians began farming. When raids occurred in southern Arizona shortly afterward, Tucson citizens protested to General Stoneman. The general replied that he had his orders from Washington and must obey them. But, he said, the local citizens were not so bound and must therefore rely on themselves. This cryptic remark possibly accounted for what followed. Under the fiery leadership of William Saunders Oury, a Tucson lawyer, a citizen army from Tucson, composed of six Americans, forty-eight Mexicans, and ninety-four Papago Indians, slipped out of town and proceeded to Aravaipa Canyon. At dawn on April 30 the party attacked, taking the Aravaipa Apaches by surprise. One hundred women and children and eight men were killed. Twenty-nine children were captured and taken to Tucson as slaves. The affair caused a good deal of excitement in the east, where it was labeled the "Camp Grant Massacre." The participants were arrested and brought to trial, but a local jury found them not guilty. Arizonans would not convict a man for killing an Indian, even though the Indian might be a child —"Nits make lice," they said. Certainly the incident provided no inducement for other Indians to surrender and allow themselves to be placed on the reservation. It definitely hindered the effort to end the Indian wars peacefully.

As a result of the national attention focused on the Apache problem in Arizona by the Camp Grant Massacre, President Grant sent a peace commission to the territory. Headed by a mild-mannered Quaker, Vincent Colyer, this commission was charged with arranging treaties with the various Apache bands and with other renegade tribes, treaties reducing the hostiles to reservations. Governor A. P. K. Safford reflected public sentiment in the territory when he issued a proclamation asking the people to co-operate with the commission despite its members' "erroneous opinions upon the Indian question and the condition of affairs in the Territory." Newspaper editors were not so circumspect in their remarks, one editorial declaring that Arizonans "ought, in justice to our murdered dead, to dump the old devil [Colyer] into the shaft of some mine, and pile rocks upon him until he is dead. A rascal who comes here to thwart the efforts of military and civilians to conquer a peace from our savage foe, deserves to be stoned to death, like the treacherous, black-hearted dog that he is."

Much of this opposition was fostered by a group of merchants living in the Old Pueblo who were known as the Tucson Ring. For them Indian wars were good business. At such times, more troops were sent to Arizona, which meant that rations were purchased locally, along with grain and hay for the horses. Beyond this, they connived with Indian agents to furnish substandard rations at standard prices on the reservations, splitting the profits. Sometimes, with the connivance of such agents, they furnished no rations at all and pocketed the money. Their newspapers promoted difficulties, ran stories of atrocities, and, in general, did all they could to prevent a just peace.

Colyer nevertheless proceeded with his work, persuading some four thousand Indians to settle on reservations. At his departure the only tribes still on the warpath were the Chiricahua Apaches, parts of the Mescalero, Pinal, and Coyotero Apaches, and some of the Yavapais. While Colyer was thus occupied, General Stoneman had been transferred. Arizonans were delighted, thinking they had secured his departure through their protests. Replacing Stoneman as commander was Lieutenant Colonel George Crook, a West Point graduate and a major general during the Civil War. Before Crook could take the field, following Colyer's departure, still another peace commission arrived from Washington, this one headed by Brigadier General Oliver Otis Howard, a one-armed veteran of the Civil War known as "Bible-Quoting Howard" and "The Christian General."

Howard inspected the military posts in the department, and he moved the Camp Grant Agency northward to the Gila River, where it was renamed San Carlos. Thereafter San Carlos would be the major Apache reservation. Despite local opposition to his efforts, Howard also held a number of meetings with the renegades and with the Pimas, Papagos, and reservation Apaches. But his greatest accomplishment was a confrontation with Cochise. Thomas J. Jeffords, a white man who had won the friendship of Cochise and reportedly was a "blood brother" to the Chiricahua chief, arranged for Howard to meet Cochise. "The Christian General" went alone and unarmed to this meeting and there hammered out a verbal agreement. The Chiricahuas were given their own reservation, fifty-five miles square, in southeastern Arizona, including the Dragoon and Chiricahua Mountains and the Sulphur Springs and San Simon valleys—their traditional homeland. Tom Jeffords became the Chiricahua agent, and Cochise kept the peace.

When Howard departed, Crook was permitted to take the field against the remaining renegades. Wearing a weather-beaten canvas suit and a Japanese summer hat, with no military trappings of any style, not even a symbol of his rank, Crook quickly discarded standard army tactics. A study of conditions in Arizona convinced him that only an army capable of rapid pursuit could cope with the Indians, and he trained his men in this fashion, using mules to carry provisions and operating in extremely mobile, small units. He also decided that the best trackers of Indians were other Indians, and thus was born his Apache Scouts: Indians who were enlisted as soldiers for six months and paid standard army wages. By the fall of 1872 he was ready to test his theories in combat.

Tracking renegade Yavapais to their Date Creek Reservation, Crook narrowly escaped death at a peace conference. When the Yavapais failed to kill "Gray Fox," as they called Crook, by treachery, they fled to hideouts in canyons of the Santa Maria River. Crook and his troops pursued them, killing or capturing those in the vicinity. There followed a campaign of encirclement designed to clear the Tonto Basin area of runaway renegade Apaches. On December 28, 1872, the Battle of Skull Cave was fought. Apaches hid in a cave at the Salt River Canyon, where some sixty troops found them. The soldiers demanded that the Indians surrender but met with resistance. The Americans opened fire on the ceiling and ricocheted their shots down on the Indians. When all shooting by the Indians ceased, Major W. H. Brown led his troops inside to find some seventy-five Indians dead and thirty-five wounded. Next came a battle at Turret Butte where Crook and his troops, guided by Indian scouts, attacked and broke Tonto Apache resistance. In the spring of 1873, Crook saw his policies vindicated by the surrender of twenty-three hundred hostiles. The Indian wars were ended, and Crook was rewarded for his efforts by a startling promotion from lieutenant colonel to brigadier general.

The battles over, Crook continued to innovate. On the reservation he issued every Indian a numbered tag so that a quick count could be taken and reservation jumpers identified easily. Then in 1875 he was transferred north to fight the Sioux. Just as he was leaving, and contrary to his advice, most Apaches were brought together at San Carlos. They were crowded, with some four thousand of them living where eight hundred once had made their homes. Moreover, there were strong hatreds between the various subtribes that made proximity unwise. Placed in charge of this potential powder keg was John P. Clum, just twenty-three years old. Taking charge on August 8, 1874, Agent Clum tried to train the Apaches in self-government. He organized an Indian police force, set up a court in which Apaches presided as judge and jury, and asked that all soldiers be removed from San Carlos.

Clum's task was made still more difficult by the accession to San Carlos of all Chiricahua bands in 1876–77, but the fiery young administrator wanted all Apaches concentrated under his control. On May 8, 1876, he was ordered to close the Chiricahua Reservation and move Cochise's band to San Carlos. These Indians had been under the nominal leadership of Taza, son of Cochise, since the great chief's death in 1874, but actually they recognized no man as chief, preferring to plunder in Mexico with renegades who never had been on a reservation. On June 12, Clum, Taza, and 325 Chiricahuas made the move to San Carlos while cavalry units scouted for the renegades. More than 400 Chiricahuas fled southward under the leadership of Juh and Nolgee. These renegades roamed northern Mexico where they plundered, stealing horses and mules for sale in New Mexico and then stealing livestock north of the border for sale in Sonora and Chihuahua. Frequently they went to the Warm Springs Apache Reservation near Ojo Caliente, New Mexico, to get free rations.

On March 20, 1877, Clum received orders from the commissioner of Indian affairs to go to the New Mexican reservation to arrest ringleaders of the renegades: Gordo, Ponce, and a troublesome young war leader named Geronimo. Using his Indian police, Clum on April 22 apprehended the principal renegades, including Geronimo, and started them to San Carlos in chains. At the last moment, however, Clum was advised by telegraph that the Warm Springs Reservation was to be closed and thus he was to take 343 Warm Springs Apaches to San Carlos also. The Warm Springs chieftain, Victorio, escaped with a small band, however, and joined the renegades in Mexico. With the addition of the renegade Chiricahuas and the Warm Springs Apaches to those already at San Carlos, John P. Clum was king of the Apaches. He could count more than two thousand of them on his preserve, including most of the White Mountain Apaches, whom Crook had promised to leave in their homeland near Fort Apache. Although Clum relished the policy of concentration that gave him so much power, he was honest and genuinely wanted to aid the Indians. This was impractical because of bureaucratic red tape and graft in the Indian service, and Clum quarreled incessantly with his superiors. He also disliked army officers who felt they should police the reservations. In disgust with his problems, Clum resigned in August, 1877, to become a journalist.

Crook's successors as commander of the Department of Arizona had proved as unsuccessful as Crook had been successful. From 1875 to 1878, Brevet Major General August V. Kautz presided. He kept troops in the field almost constantly, but to little avail. The Apaches left the reservations almost at will—which was frequently—and quarrels with officials in Washington led to Kautz's removal in March, 1878. He was replaced by Brevet Major General Orlando B. Willcox. Under his disastrous management occurred the bloody Victorio campaign, when the Warm Springs Apaches rampaged in 1879–80, killing almost one thousand people in Arizona, New Mexico, and Chihuahua before Victorio was shot by a Mexican scalp hunter. Once again the Warm Springs Apaches were returned to San Carlos, where they united with the Chiricahuas.

The year 1881 started peacefully enough. Then in June, 1881, Nakaidoklini, a medicine man, stirred the White Mountain Apaches with a new religion. A mystic who had attended a Christian school in Santa Fe, Nakaidoklini preached the resurrection of the dead and a return to the "good old days." To achieve this, his followers were told to perform an unusual dance—a ghost dance. On August 15, a San Carlos agent, Joseph C. Tiffany informed Colonel Eugene A. Carr, commander of the Sixth Cavalry, that he wished Nakaidoklini "arrested or killed or both." Carr led seventy-nine soldiers, twenty-three scouts, and nine civilians to Cibecu Creek and on August 30 arrested the prophet of the new religion. At their encampment that evening the Americans were attacked by some one hundred followers of Nakaidoklini, and in the fighting the medicine man was slain by his guards. Carr and his soldiers were barely able to reach Fort Apache the next day, only to be attacked there on September 1 by angry White Mountain Apaches in one of the few direct attacks on an army post by Arizona Indians. Na-ti-o-tish assumed the mantle of leadership of the White Mountain Apaches, and a battle was fought between them and the soldiers at East Clear Creek on July 17, 1882. The Battle of Big Dry Wash, as it was called, resulted in the death of twenty-two Apaches and the surrender of the rest. It was the last real battle between Indian and soldier on Arizona soil.

While the ghost-dance craze was sweeping the White Mountain Apaches, the Chiricahuas had taken advantage of the diversion. Taza had died in 1876 and was succeeded by Nachez (also spelled Naiche), his younger brother. Nachez and his three leading war chiefs, Chatto, Juh, and Geronimo, fled into Mexico at the end of September, 1881. Again it was George Crook who had to secure their surrender, for he had returned to command the department on September 4, 1882. Under terms of a treaty between the United States and Mexico, signed on July 29, 1882, troops of either nation could cross the international boundary in pursuit of hostiles. Just as Crook was preparing to campaign in Sonora, Chatto stormed out of Mexico with part of the renegades in search of ammunition. Along the way the Indians murdered Judge H. C. McComas and his wife and carried off their six-year-old son Charles. Later the boy was found dead. This incident received national attention because of the prominence of the judge, and a cry was raised in the newspapers for punishment of the guilty Indians. One Chiricahua, known as Tso-ay by the Indians and Peaches by the Americans, deserted Chatto's group during the raid and tried to return to the reservation. Captured and taken to Crook for questioning, Peaches agreed to lead the soldiers to the Apache hideout in Mexico. With 45 cavalrymen and 193 Apache Scouts, Crook crossed into Sonora and surprised the hostiles at their village high in the Sierra on May 15. Eight days later, he started home with 285 prisoners, who said they were tired of war. Eventually all the hostiles in Mexico surrendered, including Geronimo, who returned with his followers in January, 1884. Once again peace had been restored, and Crook was the hero of the hour.

But no real solution to the Indian problem had been achieved. The Apaches still felt crowded at San Carlos. They also were being cheated on their rations by unscrupulous agents. Unaccustomed to farming, they could not raise enough to eat, and their food supplies were woefully short. A final humiliation came when Crook forbade their making or drinking *tiswin*, a native beer. In May, 1885, the most restless warriors determined upon a confrontation. In a mass group they came to Lieutenant Britton Davis, a young officer in immediate charge of them, and said they all had made and drunk *tiswin*. No jail was available that could hold them all, so Davis wired General Crook for instructions. His telegram was pigeonholed by a captain who did not realize its importance. More than three months passed before Crook saw it. Meanwhile, the Apaches waited for two days, growing more and more apprehensive. Finally, in panic, they fled the reservation to Mexico. Crook organized pursuit. Led, as usual, by the Apache Scouts and commanded by Captain Emmet Crawford, the American force followed into Sonora. There, in January, 1886, Crawford met with Geronimo and the renegades to arrange surrender. However, Mexican scalp hunters arrived, mistook the Apache Scouts for renegades, and began firing. Crawford tried to halt the shooting but was killed. The nearby hostiles heard this exchange of shots and fled. It was March 25, 1886, before a surrender conference was finally arranged between them and Crook.

At this meeting, which took place at Cañon de los Embudos, in Sonora, Geronimo stated to Crook, "Two or three words are enough. I have little to say. I surrender myself to you." On the way to San Carlos, however, a wandering peddler, Bob Tribollet, an employee of the Tucson Ring, sold whisky to Geronimo. He and thirty-eight followers then returned to their Sonoran mountain hideout. In the outcry that followed, Crook was forced to resign as commander of the department. His replacement, Brigadier General Nelson A. Miles, was a former crockery clerk from Boston who had made a reputation during the Civil War. He had spent thousands of dollars on a heliograph system that never resulted in a battle or a captive. With almost five thousand troops at his command, Miles tried to force the Apaches into an unconditional surrender. When that failed, he turned to Crook's policy of a negotiated surrender. This was arranged by Lieutenant Charles B. Gatewood, who went unarmed into Geronimo's camp in Sonora guided by two friendly Apache Scouts. The surrender formally took place at Skeleton Canyon in southern Arizona on September 4, 1886, when Geronimo met with Miles. The general promised the Apaches they would be kept prisoner in Florida for two years, then returned to Arizona. Going with the Apaches into exile in Florida were the two friendly Apaches who had guided Gatewood to Geronimo's camp, and also sent to Florida were all Chiricahua and Warm Springs Apaches. These Apaches were held prisoners of war until 1913—and were never returned to Arizona. In 1888 they were moved from Florida to Alabama and in 1894 to the Indian Territory (Oklahoma).

By 1886 the Indians of Arizona had become a political and social problem, not a military one. They had been defeated and confined on reservations and no longer were a threat to life and property. Occasionally one of them would make trouble—as the Apache Kid did in the 1890's —but such renegades were outlaws in the traditional western sense, not brave leaders of a defiant people. The Indians on the reservations were encouraged by national legislation, such as the Dawes Act of 1887 and the Burke Act of 1906, to take 160 acres, to become citizens and farmers, and in short to be anything but Indians. Their reservation land comprised some 27 per cent of the Territory of Arizona, and there they were provided health services and generally supervised by the Bureau of Indian Affairs. No longer were they masters of Arizona. They had become its stepchildren.

Arizona Bonanzas

Mining in Arizona, which virtually had ceased at the outbreak of the Civil War, was greatly stimulated by the arrival of the California Column in 1862. Many of the volunteers who arrived with General Carleton had prospected in California, and they brought with them their dreams of striking it rich. Even Carleton had such hopes, for he granted permits to prospect in northern Arizona, permits reportedly carrying an unwritten agreement that he would share in what was found. Strikes were made, significantly in northern and western Arizona; elsewhere the hand that ruled the territory was Apache. Gold had been discovered at Gila City, twenty miles upriver from Yuma, in 1858, and it continued to be mined there after the Civil War began. It was logical that new strikes would be sought in that vicinity. Gold was found in small quantities up the Colorado River from Yuma, giving rise to Olive City and Mineral City, towns that eventually would become part of Ehrenberg. Early the following year, 1863, A. H. Peeples, Jack Swilling, and Paulino Weaver made a strike at Antelope Hill in the Weaver Mountains. In some three months, approximately $100,000 in nuggets, varying in size from a speck to a hickory nut, were found at the depression on Antelope Hill.

Nearby Henry Wickenburg, another veteran of the California Column, discovered what came to be known as the Vulture Mine, located ten miles south of the town that today bears his name. However, water was distant, and Wickenburg did not have the funds to develop his find. He sold the Vulture for $85,000—and lost a fortune— for eventually the Vulture yielded $3,000,000 in gold. Other discoveries, including that by the Joseph Reddeford Walker party at Prescott, were made in 1863–64. Creek names in that vicinity—such as the Hassayampa, the Big Bug, Lynx, Turkey, and Agua Fria—became well known among the mining fraternity all across the West, but by 1864 much of the surface minerals had been extracted, and the excitement dwindled.

The next discovery to attract outsiders' attention was the Silver King, which originated in road construction started in 1871. That year General George Stoneman ordered a military road built to Picket Post Butte, which was used as a lookout and signal station. A soldier named Sullivan, employed in cutting the trail, found a piece of heavy black ore as he worked. Later, his term of enlistment up, he moved to Florence, where he showed the piece of ore frequently. For the next two years local citizens hunted "Sullivan's Mine," the former soldier having died without revealing the location. In 1875, four farmers and ranchers from Florence on a trip from Globe to their homes camped one night at the foot of Stoneman's Grade. The next morning one of them, Isaac Copeland, found rich ore. Copeland, Benjamin W. Reagan, William H. Long, and Charles G. Mason agreed to a four-way split, and they filed a location notice on the Silver King Mine.

None of the four really knew anything about mining. When they packed their first shipment of ore to a San Francisco smelter, they threw the good silver ore into the dump and carefully packed poor ore. That first shipment netted them a $12,000 loss. Discouraged, they offered the mine to a merchant as payment on their account at his store. He refused. At this juncture, four miners from Nevada who were traveling through the region saw the rich "dump" and made an arrangement to work the dump for half the profits they could derive from it. Their first shipment netted a profit of $50,000. James Barney, a Yuma merchant, began negotiations to purchase the Silver King. Copeland sold his quarter-interest for $30,000. Long demanded and received $100,000. Then, by buying part of the shares owned by Mason and Reagan, Barney had control of the mine. He incorporated the Silver King under California laws on May 8, 1877. Within nine years the mine once refused by a storekeeper as payment for a small bill had produced more than $6,000,000 in silver.

The granddaddy of all Arizona mines came next, the strike by Ed Schieffelin. A child of the gold rush of forty-nine, Schieffelin had gone west as a lad with his father and had grown to manhood prospecting in Oregon, Nevada, Utah, and Idaho. But in 1875, when he visited his father in California, he had only $2.50 to show for his years of wandering. He decided that his mistake was rushing in where others had made a strike, that on his next trip he would search where no one had found anything. Borrowing $100 from his father as a grubstake, he set out in the spring of 1877 for southeastern Arizona. In company with soldiers scouting in that vicinity (who would establish Fort Huachuca), he arrived at the San Pedro River not far from the international boundary. During the day, while the troops scouted for renegade Apaches, Schieffelin combed the hills for "float"—pieces of ore that had broken off from the main deposit (the mother lode) and had been washed down into the valleys by rains. Every evening, when he returned to the soldiers' camp for protection, the troops would ask, "Have you found anything?" Schieffelin would reply, "No, not yet," to which the soldiers would respond, "All you will find here is your tombstone." He did find some specimens containing silver, specimens he took to Tucson in search of a financial backer. Tucsonans advised him to try ranching, saying that there was nothing in southeastern Arizona.

Still he persisted, but by October, 1877, his supplies were exhausted. Taking his best specimens, he went in search of his brother Al, who was working at the McCracken Mine to the north. Al was unexcited by his brother's claims but agreed to getting an assayer's report. Richard Gird assayed the samples, found them rich, and asked to go to the area where they had been found. Finally an agreement was made between the three to a partnership, a share-and-share-alike agreement. In February, 1878, the three departed for southeastern Arizona. Stopping in Tucson, Gird persuaded John S. Vosburg, a gun merchant in the Old Pueblo and a secret partner of Governor A. P. K. Safford in grubstaking mining ventures, to invest in the project. Vosburg supplied them with $300 credit. Proceeding to the point where Schieffelin had found his samples, they began their search. That first area they called "The Grave-yard," for there, they said, they buried their hopes. It proved a disappointment. But Ed Schieffelin persuaded the other two to remain in the vicinity for a time, and soon they developed a routine. Ed and Al would search for samples while Gird ran assays on the previous day's pieces. After several weeks' work, Ed Schieffelin finally found the lode—which assayed at $9,000 to the ton of ore. Quickly they filed claim on several rich prospects.

Vosburg, when informed of the strike, notified former Governor Safford, who brought the Corbin brothers of Connecticut to Arizona. Their inspection convinced them that silver indeed had been found. They advanced $80,000 to finance a quartz mill, hire miners, and begin operations, for which they received a one-eighth share; Safford and Vosburg also received a one-eighth share; Gird and the Schieffelins each held one-quarter interest in the Tombstone Mining and Milling Company. The company paid $50,000 a month in dividends for twenty-seven months—until the Corbin brothers bought out the Schieffelins, Gird, and Safford. Only Vosburg retained an interest.

Other mines were discovered in the vicinity. The result was a town named by Schieffelin—Tombstone. John Clum founded a newspaper which he called, fittingly, the *Epitaph*. By 1882 the town had an estimated population of fifteen thousand and was the largest city between San Antonio and San Francisco. The silver output from the mines rescued Arizona from economic depression, caused the Southern Pacific to choose a southern route through Arizona, and attracted ranchers and farmers to Arizona. By 1888 more than $30,000,000 had been extracted in this area, but the bonanza did not last much longer. In one of the most arid parts of the state the problem was water—

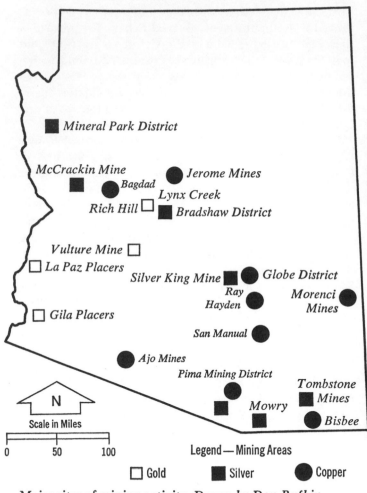

Major sites of mining activity. *Drawn by Don Bufkin*

flooding of the mines at about five hundred feet. Expensive pumping systems failed to solve the problem, and mining ceased. By 1901 fewer than one thousand people were left in Tombstone. That same year a co-operative effort by all the mine owners to install pumps was more successful, and rich ore again brought a revival to the town. But in 1909 at about one thousand feet down, flooding halted work a second and final time.

Mining continued on a greatly reduced scale at Tombstone well into the twentieth century, and new discoveries have been made in the vicinity in very recent years. The total value of mineral production is beyond $80,000,000, the early money coming at a time when Arizona badly needed it. In addition, the mines at Tombstone attracted workers who, when flooding deprived them of their jobs, moved north to the copper mines and provided a source of skilled labor. Tombstone's significance was not the violent outlaws it attracted but its economic impact.

Less dramatic but equally significant to Arizona's economic development in the late 1870's and early 1880's was Harshaw, some fifty miles to the west. The mine discovered in 1877 by David Tecumseh Harshaw, a veteran of the California Column, was acquired in 1879 by the Hermosa Mining Company of New York. The following year the company began a major operation at the mine and town bearing Harshaw's name. With a reduction mill in operation, the mine produced $365,654 in silver in just four months. Buildings of adobe, of stone, and of timber were constructed, a school was opened, and a newspaper and several businesses established, and Harshaw was advertised as a city of ten thousand residents. But the boom quickly passed, leaving behind another ghost town to dot the mountains of Arizona.

Silver—the major precious metal in Arizona—declined in value in the 1880's owing to national conditions, and mining gradually faded as a major source of income for the territory. Between 1884 and 1893 silver was not coined nationally, and its value declined steadily. Gold mining did flourish again briefly in Arizona with the invention in 1891 of the cyanide process of extracting gold from ore, replacing the older and more costly process.

One of the most colorful features of Arizona mining was the number of swindles it engendered. Perhaps the most ambitious was the product of the fertile mind of Dr. Richard C. Flower, a New York City quack. In 1899, when he heard that a strip of the old San Carlos Reservation would be opened to mining, Flower advertised "Spenazuma Mining Company" stock at $10.00 a share, claiming to have found gold. His advertisements had a gold border with nuggets hanging from the word "Spenazuma" as if ready to fall into the lap of anyone who purchased shares. With the funds derived from the sale of stock, Flower announced a dividend—and the price of a share of his stock rose to $12.00 and beyond. Then George H. Smalley, a reporter for the Phoenix *Arizona Republican* began investigating, for he realized the San Carlos area was rich in silver but not in gold. Despite threats to his life—and a few shots taken at him—he proved the operation a swindle. Flower was brought to trial and eventually served a prison sentence.

Despite such promotions, Arizona's rich potential of precious metals attracted prospectors during the last years of the nineteenth century. Some of these men found gold and silver, but most moved on to comb the hills in other states and territories. Yet the strikes that were made had contributed significantly to the economic development of the region. Towns were built, schools and churches established along with courthouses and jails, ranches and farms dotted the countryside to feed the miners, and in the process Arizona changed from a frontier to a stable part of the West.

THE TRANSPORTATION REVOLUTION

The Civil War had brought an end to the Butterfield Overland Mail, and Arizona was left without commercial transportation to the outside world. The first stages to rumble and bounce across the territory after that war came in 1869 when the Southern Overland U. S. Mail and Express connected Tucson with Mesilla and the East. The following year the Tucson, Arizona City, and San Diego Stage Company re-established service to the West Coast, and southern Arizona once again assumed an air of importance, of economic growth. Miners found ready transportation available to them, although not very comfortable. Stage transportation spread with the growth of boom mining towns as each, soon after its founding, was provided with stage service by enterprising operators. For example, the Tucson and Tombstone Express, established by J. D. Kinnear, began operating in mid-November of 1878 to serve that community with weekly connections with the Old Pueblo—at a healthy profit to Kinnear.

The king of the freighting industry in Arizona, prior to the arrival of the railroads, was the firm of Tully and Ochoa. Estevan Ochoa, born in Chihuahua City in 1831, moved to Tucson in the spring of 1860, established a freighting firm, and, after merging with P. R. Tully about 1864, came to own wagons and teams valued at $100,000. They employed hundreds of men who hauled goods from as far away as Kansas City, and they dominated the supplying of government posts and reservations. The firm fought Indians, hard times, and hard men—but it could not fight the railroad, which could freight supplies at a fraction of Tully and Ochoa's costs. When the "iron horse" arrived, the firm began to diminish in size.

The Colorado River continued to be an important artery of commerce during the post–Civil War period—and even after the arrival of the railroad. George A. Johnson's firm, as before the war, was the most successful such operation. The name was changed to the Colorado Steam Navigation Company, and it operated as such until it was purchased by the Southern Pacific Railroad in 1878. The Colorado was a perilous and vexatious river, filled with shifting sandbars and submerged snags. There always was the problem of fuel, for the boats on the Colorado burned wood, and the captains were dependent on the good will and labor of the Indians to keep them supplied. Finally, this mode of travel was not comfortable. Martha Summerhayes, an army wife, described her journey on the *Gila* in 1874 in less than generous terms: "We had staterooms, but could not remain in them long at a time, on account of the intense heat. . . . After a hasty meal, and a few remarks upon the salt beef, and the general misery of our lot, we would seek some spot which might be a trifle cooler. . . . Conversation lagged; no topic seemed to have any interest except the thermometer, which hung in the coolest place on the boat; and one day when Major Worth looked at it and pronounced it 122° in the shade, a grim despair seized upon me." Boats were plying the waters of the Colorado as late as 1908, but the building of the mighty dams ended a romantic chapter of Arizona's transportation history.

Perhaps the greatest event in Arizona in the nineteenth

century was the arrival of the railroads. There had been talk of transcontinental railroads since the 1840's, and federal surveys had been conducted in 1853–54. But nothing came of such efforts until after the Civil War, when work began in earnest. The federal government offered inducements to the building of transcontinental railroads which made them attractive financial risks, such as twenty free sections of land for each mile of track laid and a loan of $16,000 for each mile of track laid in level country, $32,000 for each mile in the foothills, and $48,000 for each mile in the mountains (this loan constituting a second mortgage). The first charter to build across the Southwest was granted by Congress on July 27, 1866, to the Atlantic and Pacific Railroad. This line was to be built from Springfield, Missouri, to Albuquerque, New Mexico, and thence westward along the thirty-fifth parallel "as near as may be found most suitable for a railway route" to the Colorado River and the Pacific Coast. The Atlantic and Pacific failed to make giant strides after it was chartered, and the company collapsed in the Panic of 1873. The other major charter involving Arizona went on March 3, 1871, to the Texas and Pacific Railway, which was to run from the East Texas village of Marshall along the thirty-second parallel westward to San Diego. At the time of the Panic of 1873 the Texas and Pacific had reached Dallas. Neither line was making satisfactory progress.

Other companies, more capable of laying track, took advantage of the slowness of the Texas and Pacific and the Atlantic and Pacific. The "Big Four" of California railroading—Mark Hopkins, Collis P. Huntington, Leland Stanford, and Charles Crocker—were determined to achieve a monopoly on railroad routes to their state. They secured a charter for the Southern Pacific from a compliant California legislature and began building down the coast from San Francisco to San Diego. Spur lines were laid eastward from the main route of this road to Needles and to Yuma Crossing; as these were the only satisfactory entrances to California for possible competition, they thus assured themselves that any competitors would have to make arrangements with them. At Fort Yuma, the Southern Pacific came to a halt, blocked both by the need for a federal permit to build across the military reservation of Fort Yuma and by the fact that the Texas and Pacific had the charter providing subsidies to build across Arizona and New Mexico. They likewise were blocked at Needles by the charter of the Atlantic and Pacific.

Collis P. Huntington, president of the Southern Pacific, was not content to wait for the Texas and Pacific to reach Yuma Crossing. In 1877 he secured permission from Congress to build across the Fort Yuma military reservation, and that same year he persuaded the legislature of Arizona to grant permission to build across that territory. Work then was hurried, and the end-of-track moved eastward. On March 20, 1880, the Southern Pacific was at Tucson, where a gala celebration was held. Charles Crocker, then president of the Southern Pacific, was at the Old Pueblo for the ceremony of driving the last spike. Richard Gird provided a silver spike, shaped from the first bullion produced by the Tough Nut Mine in Tombstone, for the occasion—highly fitting, for it was the discovery of Tombstone's silver mines that persuaded Southern Pacific officials to build to Tucson rather than proceed up the Gila River basin to New Mexico. Building on eastward, the railroad went through Benson, Willcox, and Bowie, thence to Lordsburg, Deming, and Las Cruces, New Mexico, to El Paso, Texas. It connected with the Texas and

Pacific at Sierra Blanca, some ninety miles east of El Paso, on January 1, 1882. When Congress refused to endorse a transfer of the Texas and Pacific land grant to the Southern Pacific, that line acquired the Galveston, Harrisburg, and San Antonio Railroad and eventually reached New Orleans. The first transcontinental line across Arizona had been completed.

Meanwhile, the Atchison, Topeka, and Santa Fe was building. Under the direction of Cyrus K. Holliday, the Santa Fe (as it was called) had built from Kansas to New Mexico early in the 1880's. Holliday originally had hoped to build west from New Mexico to California by way of the thirty-second parallel, but the hasty construction of the Southern Pacific prevented his doing this. The Santa Fe did connect with the Southern Pacific at Deming, New Mexico, allowing Santa Fe cars to reach California, but Holliday wanted his own line all the way to the Pacific— and the charter originally granted to the Atlantic and Pacific was still good. Attempts to reorganize the Atlantic and Pacific in 1876 had been unsuccessful, and it was easily acquired by the Santa Fe (which would operate it as a subsidiary until 1897 when it would be amalgamated with the parent company). In May, 1880, the Santa Fe began building westward, thereby gaining title to the ten-million-acre subsidy. Northern Arizona proved difficult to cross, but by August, 1883, the end-of-track was at the Colorado River just across from Needles, California. In the process of building across Arizona, several railhead towns had been created, many of them named for Santa Fe officials: Winslow, Holbrook, Flagstaff, Williams, Ash Fork, Seligman, and Kingman. On August 20, 1884, the Santa Fe concluded a purchase agreement with the Southern Pacific, whereby the Santa Fe acquired title to the

Needles-Mojave line. Connections were then made for right-of-way on to San Diego, which was reached on November 14, 1885—and a second transcontinental railroad across Arizona had been completed.

As each of these lines crossed the territory, ramshackle railhead towns sprang into existence to house the families of Irish, Chinese, and other immigrant workers who drove the spikes and carried the ties, the merchants who came to supply their goods, and the gamblers, saloon-keepers, and "soiled doves" who came to separate them from their pay. Shanty towns similar to the mining boom camps, these railhead towns were of canvas and raw lumber. Each had its brief moment of glory and then quickly regressed to the status of sleepy frontier village when the track moved on. They were not as dreary as frequently pictured, however: each generally boasted fine restaurants, an opera house for touring theatrical groups, churches, and even schools within a very short period of time. They became stable towns when the rowdy element moved on to the next end-of-track town.

The remainder of the railroading story is one of building connecting lines between the transcontinentals and of short lines to outlying villages and mines. For example, a subsidiary of the Santa Fe built from Ash Fork, a town serviced by the Santa Fe, southward to Phoenix in the 1890's and connected with the Southern Pacific at Maricopa. Eventually almost every major town in the territory had rail service, just as did every major mine. William S. Oury summed up the impact of the railroad in his speech in Tucson on March 20, 1880, when he declared, "We now have no frontier to which the pioneer may flee to avoid the tramp of civilized progress."

LONGHORNS WEST

Ranching in Arizona, as an occupation, had strong Spanish antecedents. Kino and the Jesuits introduced the longhorn to the missions shortly after their founding, and soon there were immense mission herds. The Franciscans continued this work. Civilians likewise found conditions in Arizona suitable for grazing the longhorn. However, there was the Indian menace which interfered strongly. Nicolás de Lafora, the engineer who accompanied the Marqués de Rubí on his tour of inspection in 1767, spoke of many ranches in southern Arizona abandoned because of Indian depredations. Ranching flourished again during the years of peace at the end of Spanish control. In the Mexican period, Governor Gándara of Sonora owned Tumacácori and ran thousands of sheep on that land. But ranching while the Apaches roamed at will was a desperate business, and many haciendas were abandoned for that reason. For example, Lieutenant Colonel Philip St. George Cooke and the Mormon Battalion found San Bernardino (in extreme southeastern Arizona) deserted and the cattle running wild in 1846. At the time of the American conquest, few cattle were wearing brands in Arizona.

Cattle next came to Arizona as a result of the California gold rush. During the mad scramble to California, prices for beef skyrocketed to the extent that longhorns from Texas were driven to the gold fields. From South Texas, where cattle had flourished, herds were gathered in 1848–49 and driven west across New Mexico and Arizona to the new El Dorado where they brought one hundred dollars a head on the hoof. Enterprising Sonorans, such as Jesús and José Redondo, who later built a large ranching operation near Yuma, brought cattle and sheep from their home state to California to take advantage of the high prices.

Probably the first ranch to be established in Arizona following the American conquest was that of William Kirkland, who reportedly brought a herd from Mexico in 1857—some two hundred head—which he used to establish the Canoa Ranch. Located on the Santa Cruz River thirty-five miles south of Tucson and twenty miles north of Tubac, this venture prospered to the extent that others were encouraged to try ranching. William S. Oury purchased one hundred cattle in 1858 from a drover bound from Illinois to California, with which he stocked a ranch just south of Tucson. Later he moved to Tanque Verde east of the Old Pueblo. Pete Kitchen, who farmed just north of present-day Nogales, likewise kept cattle, although he is best remembered for his hogs.

The coming of the Civil War almost completely halted ranching operations in Arizona, however. With the soldiers removed eastward, cattlemen had little or no protection from marauding Indians. With the end of the war, new markets opened which made ranching again attractive, despite the Indian threat which continued until the 1880's. The soldiers stationed in the territory after the war provided a ready market for beef, as did the reservations. The discoveries of gold and silver attracted miners and created boom prices for beef on the hoof. These high prices first attracted drovers from Texas and California who brought cattle raised elsewhere, but several of them stayed in Arizona to increase the number of ranchers living in the territory. Soon Arizona was not only supplying its own needs but also exporting beef elsewhere. These early cattle kings ran their cattle on the public domain, not actually owning title to the grass and water with which they fattened their animals. Some of them grew fabulously wealthy in the process.

One of the most famous of the early cattlemen to arrive in Arizona was Henry Clay Hooker, a refugee from the California gold rush. He secured his first capital by purchasing five hundred turkeys in California at $1.50 each, driving them overland to the Nevada mining camps, and selling them for $5.00 apiece. Then in 1867 he secured a contract to supply beef to army posts in northern Arizona. He purchased the cattle in Texas and Arizona and drove them to the territory. Finally, in 1872, he established his Sierra Bonita Ranch in the Sulphur Springs Valley of southern Arizona. Despite the incursions of the Chiricahua Apaches—which included one face-to-face meeting between Hooker and Cochise—the rancher persisted in his operation. Within a few years he had the largest and most successful ranch in the territory. He introduced the new breeds of cattle—shorthorns, Durhams, and Herefords—to the eight hundred square miles that he controlled. For the comfort of the many guests who stayed at the ranch, he kept a dairy herd, poultry, and a large garden. He also pioneered in breeding and racing horses noted for their stamina and their beauty.

Not far southwest from the Sierra Bonita was the Empire Ranch. Established in 1876 by Walter L. Vail, with his English partners H. R. Hislop and John Harvey, it was located in the Santa Rita Mountains and proved quite successful. Other operations in the vicinity included the San Simon Cattle Company and the San Bernardino Ranch. The latter, owned by John H. Slaughter, a Texan later noted as the sheriff who tamed Tombstone, dated from a Spanish land grant of forty thousand acres of which only some ten thousand acres were in Arizona; the rest was south of the border.

Ranching was not confined to southern Arizona alone. To the west, near Yuma, José and Jesús Redondo ran herds over a range of some one hundred square miles, supplying beef to the army and to the work crews of the Southern Pacific. And Yavapai County in northern Arizona became noteworthy for its many fine ranches. William Wingfield began applying his "Hatchet" brand to cattle in the Verde Valley about 1881. The largest operation in northern Arizona, however, was corporate. In 1883 the Aztec Land and Cattle Company secured a range some forty by ninety miles in size from the Atlantic and Pacific Railroad and began running about sixty thousand head of cattle on it. With headquarters on the Little Colorado River near Joseph City, the "Hashknife" (as it was known) was plagued by absentee ownership and rustling. Captain Burt Mossman, later an Arizona Ranger of note, was hired to superintend the operation, but even such a man as he could not halt the rustling, and the operation ceased about 1900.

Ranching began to change during the 1880's in Arizona as elsewhere. With transcontinental railroads completed, thus opening the market to eastern packing plants, a boom period came to the territory. Staid Bostonians vied with gouty squires from England to invest in western ranches, and Arizona land values rose rapidly. More and still more cattle grazed the ranges. The result was inevitable—overgrazing. At the same time, barbed wire and the windmill made possible the closing of the open range as farmers began homesteading the land. The ranchers could fight the Indians and the rustlers who preyed on them, but they could not fight the technological progress that brought thousands of farmers. Then came the disastrous winter of 1886–87 which froze cattle from Canada to Texas. Although this blizzard did not hit Arizona, it depressed the national cattle market to such an extent that it hit the pocketbook and bank account of every rancher in the territory.

Faced with Indian difficulties, rustlers, homesteaders, and a depressed market, Arizona's ranchers were forced to organize. In 1884 they founded a territorial cattlemen's association. This organization lobbied for quarantine laws to prevent the introduction of Texas Fever (carried by ticks), and it pressured the territorial legislature to create the Livestock Sanitary Board, which became a reality in 1887. But drought—three dry years in 1885–87 followed in 1892 by a prolonged dry season—was what finally forced real changes in Arizona ranching. Wells were drilled, fences built, and new breeds of cattle introduced. The romantic days were gone. Modern ranching became the way of life despite the wry comments of old-timers who swore the longhorn was the best ranch animal.

Sheep likewise were introduced in large numbers to Arizona just after the Civil War. Navahos had stolen tens of thousands of these animals from Spaniards and Mexicans in New Mexico, and they had grazed in Arizona for two centuries when the boom period of ranching began. Then, in 1866, Juan Candelaria brought a flock westward from Cubero, New Mexico, to Apache County at the site of present-day Concho. Although Arizonans had no real taste for mutton, Candelaria did find some market for meat, and the price of wool proved far steadier than that of beef. James Baker of California drove sheep into Yavapai County in 1868, while Isadore Solomon introduced the "woolies" to Graham County that same year. In 1873–

74 drought in California forced many sheepmen to bring their animals to Arizona, and Flagstaff became their major city. Some of these sheepmen rivaled the cattlemen in the size of their domains and the number of their animals. For example, the Daggs brothers at one time were running more than fifty thousand head of sheep. Mormon settlers near Tuba City and Sunset City likewise were running large numbers of sheep and had woolen mills operating at the two settlements. The railroad proved an even greater stimulus to sheep-raisers than to the cattlemen, for it opened eastern markets for their mutton. By the early 1880's, there was growing contention between the cattlemen and the sheepmen for grazing lands.

The most noteworthy fight between these two factions came in 1887 at Tonto Basin. The Graham-Tewksbury Feud, known also as the Pleasant Valley War, erupted when the Tewksburys moved sheep owned by the Daggs brothers of Flagstaff south of the Mogollon Rim into the Tonto Basin. Many of the settlers in the region, cattlemen, joined the Grahams in opposing this move, and shooting began. The war lasted five years and the sheep were driven out of the basin, but not before twenty-nine men died— every male Graham was killed while only Ed Tewksbury survived from his family.

Despite such violence and opposition, sheepmen persisted in their efforts. In 1886 at Flagstaff they organized the Arizona Sheep Breeders and Wool Growers Association, which proved an effective lobby for their interests. By 1891 their members owned 700,000 head of sheep and marketed 5,000,000 pounds of wool annually. But it was not numbers or organization that brought peace to Arizona's grazing industry. Both had similar interests in fighting the homesteaders. Both could fight the National Forest

movement that came with conservationists' efforts to preserve natural stands of timber—but which withdrew open-
range grazing lands from use by grazers. Finally the cattlemen sought peace—even began running a few head of the
hated "woolies" themselves—when they learned that the
price of wool did not fluctuate as the price of beef did,
just as they learned that cattle and sheep would graze
contentedly on the same land. For example, in 1890 when
the price of beef had fallen disastrously, wool was selling
steadily at twenty-five cents a pound.

During the hard times of the 1890's, rustling grew to
such proportions that honest ranchers were facing bankruptcy through that source alone. Galeyville, in southeastern Cochise County, was a major rendezvous for the
rustlers who stole cattle in Arizona and sold them in
Mexico, while at the same time they stole cattle in Mexico
for sale to Arizona ranchers unconcerned with foreign
brands and an absence of title papers. Lobbying by the
cattlemen's association brought the creation, in 1901, of
the Arizona Rangers, a force of peace officers commanded
by Burt Mossman. He was succeeded by Thomas H. Ryn-
ning, who in turn was succeeded by Harry Wheeler. These
three men and their followers were able to stop the rustling
because they were tough men who could ride and shoot—
and who were not unduly bothered by crossing south of
the border (where they had no authority) to make arrests.

Shortly after the turn of the twentieth century, ranching
in Arizona had assumed its modern proportions. Fenced
pastures with windmills turning contained large herds
of Herefords and Angus cattle, frequently with sheep
grazing alongside them. Rails carried the cattle to market
in Los Angeles and Kansas City, as well as to local markets.
Cowboys laid aside their guns when the cattle barons

began buying their acres and fencing them. Hot, dirty, hard work for forty dollars a month and keep became the lot of the cowboy, who, although not as picturesque as his romanticized version in the movies, nevertheless did much to civilize Arizona and transform the character of the land.

THE FARMING FRONTIER

Prior to the Civil War there was relatively little farming in Arizona. A few small plots, mainly vegetable gardens, were cultivated along the Santa Cruz River using irrigation techniques introduced by Father Kino and the Spaniards. The one notable exception to this rule was Pete Kitchen, who raised crops of wheat on his ranch north of Nogales. After the Civil War the lowly homesteaders began to compete with the cattle barons for acres, particularly in the river valleys where water was located—and where the grass grew tallest. Nor was the "nester" content to work the open range. He wanted title to his land before clearing, plowing, and planting it. The farmer was far more concerned with land laws than the miner or rancher, and he and his fellows used all their influence to protect their land and to secure more water for it.

The first land grants in Arizona came from the Spanish crown. Under the laws of Spain, all the New World was classed as "conquered territory," which meant that it belonged to the king personally. For administrative purposes under Spanish rule, Mexico in 1756 was divided into twelve areas, of which one consisted of the present Sonora, Sinaloa, and Arizona, with headquarters at Arizpe. Several grants of land were made under Spanish law, grants of immense size and ill-defined boundaries. The same loose practices continued under Mexican rule, with more large land grants being made. The Treaty of Guadalupe Hidalgo of 1848, which ended the Mexican War, and the Gadsden Purchase agreement both stipulated American recognition of existing land grants. A surveyor general's office was established in New Mexico in 1854, but owing to distance and the difficulties of the times, it did nothing about Arizona's Spanish-Mexican land grants. In 1870, John Wasson was appointed surveyor general for Arizona, and claims were filed.

Most of the claims proved very extravagant, and fraud was rampant. A total of 11,326,108 acres were claimed, but careful checking by Wasson and his successors found only 121,187 acres as legitimately granted. The largest of these was the San Ignacio del Babacomori grant; 123,068 acres were claimed by heirs, with 34,707 acres confirmed and title granted. Other large grants approved included the San Rafael, the Canoa, the San Juan de las Boquillas y Nogales, the San Bernardino, and the San José de Sonoita.

The most notorious of the claimants of Spanish-Mexican land grants was James Addison Reavis—the "Baron of Arizona." He filed for 10,467,456 acres, claiming to own a grant dating from 1758 that measured 50 by 150 miles. His barony included the present cities of Phoenix, Globe, Clifton, and Safford and extended east to the present Silver City, New Mexico. To support his outrageous claim, Reavis produced masses of faded documents, wills and papers of the Peralta family, and even a gallery of the pictures of the Peralta ancestors. He filed his first claim in his own behalf in 1883; his second claim, filed in 1885, was in behalf of Sofia Loreta Micaela de Peralta de la Córdoba, also known as Mrs. James Addison Reavis. He established the headquarters of his barony at Arizola (on the Southern Pacific a short distance east of the present

Casa Grande). There he maintained his family in state, with his two children clad in royal purple velvet. He lived at expensive hotels in New York and in Europe, spending some $60,000 a year contributed by individuals living on the land he claimed. Ten years of investigation by Land Office agents produced a sordid story of bribery, corruption, and fraud, and in 1895 Reavis was convicted on conspiracy and sentenced to six years in prison.

Another interesting case, one not involving fraud, was the Baca Float. In 1860 the United States government secured land near Las Vegas, New Mexico, from Luís María Baca. In return, he received permission to select five grants of land of 100,000 acres each, land to be nonmineral in character and vacant of settlers. Baca selected two of these floating grants in New Mexico, one in Colorado, and one in northern Arizona. The final one was selected on June 20, 1863, in southern Arizona; it included the old settlements of Tubac, Tumacacori, and Calabazas—land that had known minerals and settlers on it. The Baca Float claim was contested in the courts, finally reaching the Supreme Court of the United States in 1914 where it was upheld. Seventy families were paid by the government for their losses and moved.

Other parts of the public domain passed into private ownership by terms of the Homestead Act of 1862. This provided for 160 acres virtually free to anyone who would live on the land five years and make improvements each year. Another federal law of importance to Arizona was the Timber Culture Act of 1873, which provided a settler could have an additional 160 acres if he planted 40 acres in trees. Then in 1877 came the Desert Land Act, which was designed to aid settlers in such arid territories as

Arizona; it provided that a settler could gain title to 640 acres if he irrigated the land.

The land these Americans secured under the various land laws proved to be extremely rich. Most farming was conducted on the alluvial, sandy soil of the river valleys where anything would grow provided it had water. Arizona's long growing season was an added bonus, enabling an ambitious farmer to make at least two crops a year. Acting Governor McCormick in 1865 described the potential of Arizona: "The plow and sickle must keep company with the pick and the mill. . . . The work of the gardener and the farmer cannot fail to prove profitable, and should not be neglected." Toward the end of his speech, McCormick grew enthusiastic about the future: "As the Apache is driven back, our settlers will be able to cultivate thousands where they now occupy scores of acres, and the tame Indians will greatly increase the size of their farms. Together they will not find it difficult to supply food at low prices for a dense population, and my confidence in the future of the territory is based upon this good prospect, as much as upon the extent and excellence of its mineral resources."

The Salt River Valley would become the major area of farming in early Arizona, principally because water was available. Sylvester Mowry, an early mining promoter, had recognized this potential for in 1857 he wrote, "The whole valley of the Gila, more than four hundred miles in length, can be made with proper exertion to yield plentiful crops." Jack Swilling was the man who carried this scheme from dream to reality. Swilling, a Confederate deserter, a reputed dope addict, and a reported murderer, proved the adage that on the frontier a man was judged more by the worth of his ideas than by his reputation. In 1867, Swilling was visiting the hay camp of John Y. T. Smith, the sutler at Fort McDowell who was making a handsome profit cutting the lush grass of the Salt River Valley and selling it to the army as hay. Swilling noted regular depressions running out from the Salt River, decided that these were ruins of prehistoric Indian canals, and determined to begin irrigated farming in the valley. Raising $10,000 from such men as Henry Wickenburg and L. J. F. Jaeger, he organized the Swilling Irrigation Canal Company and began excavating the ancient canals. By the summer of 1868 crops of barley and pumpkins dotted the area. At first the little community that sprang into existence was called Pumpkinville, but by 1870 the three hundred settlers there thought the name too undignified. A mass meeting was called at which Darrel Duppa, an English exile, suggested the town be called Phoenix after the legendary bird that lived five hundred years, was consumed by fire, then was born anew from its own ashes. Duppa thought the name appropriate, for the town was growing from the ashes of an ancient civilization. The residents liked Duppa's suggestion and adopted it.

Near Phoenix in 1877 a band of Mormons founded Lehi. The following year other Mormons came, settled at Mesa, and began farming activities. But they, as well as the other residents of the valley, were troubled by the uncertain water supply. Each spring the snows in the mountains would melt, causing the rivers to flood. Then in summer the water would almost disappear just when it was most needed for irrigation. What was sorely needed, they all decided, was a dependable water supply—which meant dams. Until water was secured in sufficient, dependable, year-round quantities, farming would suffer. Patrick

Hamilton, hired by the legislature in 1881 to extol the virtues of Arizona and to promote immigration, declared, "Irrigation is the life of agriculture in the Territory. Without it scarcely anything can be raised; with it the soil is the most prolific in the west. Water, therefore, is the most precious element for the farmer in Arizona."

The answer to this riddle was canal companies. Several such operations were spawned by the success of the Swilling Irrigation Canal Company. These were joint-stock companies in which a farmer could purchase a share either with cash or by working personally to help build the diversion dam and the canals. Generally a share entitled the owner to sufficient water to raise a crop on 160 acres. In addition, he had to pay a small fee for the water he used, these funds going for repairs of the canals and for the salary of the overseer (called a *zanjero*), who distributed the water. Men considered shares in these companies wise investments, for such shares could be rented to non-owning farmers at a handsome profit each year. Operating from the Salt River, besides the Swilling Company, were the Arizona Canal Company and the Tempe Irrigating Canal Company. In fact, so many of these companies sprang into existence that disputes arose over water rights; in years of scant rainfall, some would have to do without. The water laws of the territory were surprisingly vague. The Howell Code stated, "All rivers, creeks and streams of running water in the Territory of Arizona are hereby declared public." Pioneer irrigators interpreted this statement to mean that such water was public until diverted and put to beneficial use. Then it became the property of the appropriator and did not belong to the land itself. They also contended that the first appropriator in point of time was first in point of right—that is, in years of short supply, the first appropriator of water had first right to what was available.

Arguments over water led to the famous court case *M. Wormser and the Tempe Canal Company, et al., v. The Salt River Valley Canal Company, et al.* Judge Joseph H. Kibbey presided in this dispute between two canal companies for water from the Salt River. The case, which began in 1890, lasted two years, and six thousand pages of testimony were taken before Judge Kibbey handed down his decision, which became known as the doctrine of "prior appropriation." He said, in effect, what the canal users had been asserting, that the first user of water thereafter had first right to it so long as he was making productive use of it. With their water supplies thus assured, the canal companies worked rapidly. In 1890 the amount of land under cultivation in Arizona was approximately 70,000 acres, and ten years later the amount of land being farmed had risen to 180,000 acres.

Attempts to build artificial lakes—to store water during the wet season for use when the rains did not fall—had been made several times in the early territorial years. Most such attempts, if large, met with sad results, for the dams usually were poorly constructed and were often washed away by unforeseen floods. Such was the case of Slough Reservoir, built by Mormon farmers on the Little Colorado River in 1886 at a cost of $200,000. Building dams large enough to create an effective storage lake was a very expensive undertaking—too expensive for individuals, for the canal companies, even for the meager resources of the territorial government. Buckey O'Neill, a well-known Arizona peace officer and later famous as a leader of the Rough Riders, suggested an answer in 1896 when the National Irrigation Congress met in Phoenix. O'Neill spoke in favor of a national irrigation and conservation policy financed by the federal government. Francis G. Newlands, a congressman from Nevada, subsequently introduced a bill calling for the national government to use the money derived from the sale of public lands for the construction of reclamation works. This act passed on June 17, 1902, and one of the first projects scheduled was on the Salt River.

A dam was to be placed where Tonto Creek joined the Salt River, the Tonto Basin site. Scheduled to cost $4,000,000, the dam was begun in 1905. When finally completed, it had cost $10,500,000, but included power facilities, transmission lines to Phoenix, a road from the Salt River Valley to the dam, and canals to the valley farms. Theodore Roosevelt, the President who had authorized the building of the dam, was on hand for the formal dedication on March 18, 1911. Not until four years later would the reservoir of Roosevelt Dam be filled entirely. The first water over the spillway was bottled and used to christen the battleship *Arizona*. The total capacity of the reservoir was 1,400,000 acre feet, enough to irrigate the valley below for three years. In 1917 the Salt River Valley Water Users Association was given charge of the operation of the dam and canals, and revenues were used to repay the cost of constructing the project. Such revenues totally repaid the cost of the dam by 1955.

Irrigation in Arizona thus passed through three distinct stages of development: first, by private individuals (canals, windmills, and pumps); second, by canal companies; and, third, by the federal government through its giant dams. Until the end of the nineteenth century, most irrigation fell into the first two categories. In the twentieth century the building of dams and canals grew so expensive that only the resources of the national government could provide financing. Arizona was the site of the government's pioneering effort. Roosevelt Dam was such a resounding success that such projects would be undertaken elsewhere in the territory and in the American West. But the process was just begun by the time of statehood. Arizona had still to solve its basic problem of aridity. More water was needed—which meant that the mighty Colorado River would have to be harnessed.

OUTLAWRY AND THE COMING OF JUSTICE

In 1869, A. S. Clough located a farm on two hundred acres beside Granite Creek in Yavapai County. In the next fifteen years he set out orchards and vineyards and planted wheat as well. Irrigation from Granite Creek made this development possible; he built flumes and dug canals which brought the life-giving water to his land. Then, in 1884, James E. Wing settled on land along the same creek just above Clough's farm. He too constructed flumes, ditches, and even a large dam to divert the waters of the creek to irrigate his fields and orchard. By the latter half of June, 1885, Clough found that no longer was sufficient water coming down the creek to irrigate his land. Hot words were exchanged, followed by a lawsuit. Clough hoped for relief from the courts on the basis of his prior appropriation of the water involved. In the trial that followed, held at Prescott, the jury found in favor of Clough. The judge, however, as was within his power in an equity case, disregarded the findings of the jury. He declared that Clough had stood by and watched Wing build his ditches without protest and therefore could not dispute his neighbor's claim even in dry months. Such, the judged ruled, was his interpretation of the case under the common law doctrines of England.

When the case was appealed to the Territorial Supreme Court, the verdict was reversed. W. H. Barnes, an associate justice, wrote the majority opinion. Barnes declared, "The native tribes, the Pimas and Papagoes and other Pueblo Indians, now, as they for generations have done, appropriate and use the waters of these streams in husbandry, and sacredly recognize the rights acquired by long use, and no right of a riparian owner is thought of." Not only had the Indians followed this custom, but such had been the laws of both Spain and Mexico: "Up to about a third of a century ago . . . , the territory of Arizona had been subject to the laws and customs of Mexico, and the common law had been unknown." The common law of England, Barnes emphasized, "has never been, and is not now, suited to conditions that exist here, so far as the same applies to the uses of water." Clough was entitled to first use of the water since he first appropriated it, with the exception that "no person can, by virtue of prior appropriation, claim or hold any more water than is necessary for the purpose of the appropriation."

In this one case can be seen the orderly transition from Indian to Spanish to Mexican to American control of Arizona. Indian, Spaniard, Mexican, and American alike found that harsh geographical necessity dictated laws regarding water. There was likewise no radical or abrupt break in other phases of the law as Spanish control gave way to Mexican ownership and as it in turn was supplanted by American jurisdiction. In fact, the Southwest, along with Louisiana and Florida, was the only part of the present continental United States not a lawless wilderness when the first Anglo-American pioneers arrived. In Arizona the frontiersman found a fully developed legal structure in the European sense—a heritage of three centuries of Spanish exploration, settlement, and development, a legal system based on Roman law, as opposed to the common law of England, but which had been modified to fit the necessities of life in arid Arizona.

This Spanish heritage proved very pervasive in the realm of economic endeavor. Arizona's mining, ranching, and farming (or water) laws were drawn almost totally and verbatim from the Spanish code of laws. Beyond the economic aspects of life in Arizona, Spanish law likewise had an impact on subsequent legal codes. When the Republic of Mexico came into existence in 1821, the word "Mexico" was substituted for "Spain" on the legal codes, and life went on as usual. Then, when Arizona became a part of the United States, it was made a part of the Territory of New Mexico. That territory's laws evolved from the Kearny Code, promulgated by Stephen Watts Kearny on September 22, 1846, a code, according to Kearny's own statement, which came partly from the previous laws of New Mexico, partly from the laws of Missouri, and to a lesser extent from the laws of Texas and Coahuila. Later, after territorial status was achieved in New Mexico, the legislature authorized a compilation of the laws by James J. Deavenport, an associate justice of the Territorial Supreme Court. He completed this work in 1856. Yet Arizona never felt the heavy hand of New Mexican control owing to distance and the paucity of settlers, although the New Mexican code was its official law until it became a separate territory by act of Congress in February of 1863.

The task of compiling Arizona's code of law fell to Associate Justice William T. Howell. Based largely on the laws of Michigan, New York, and California, his draft was extensively rewritten by the First Legislature to conform with conditions in Arizona—which meant that the legislators inserted many provisions stemming from Spanish law. For example, the Howell Code stressed the community property rights of women, which definitely was not English in origin. This code also established justice of the peace courts, probate courts, and district courts to work along with the Supreme Court. By 1864, Arizona had a code of laws and a court system, a smooth transition having been made from New Mexican and Mexican rule. Technically there never was a "lawless" period. But there were few requirements for sitting on a court bench, especially at the justice of the peace level; a man's knowledge of the law seemed less important to the pioneers than his desire that justice should prevail. One man who met this qualification was Charles H. Meyer of Tucson.

Meyer was a German by birth and a druggist by profession. He knew very little law when he became justice of the peace. In fact, his law library consisted of only two books: *Materia Medica* and *Fractured Bones*. At least, that was what local lawyers claimed. Yet his decisions usually were in the interests of honesty and good order and resulted in justice. It was Judge Meyer who instituted the chain-gang system in Tucson. Persons convicted in his court usually were given an opportunity to shorten their sentences by cleaning the streets of the Old Pueblo. This system pleased the people of Tucson, for it meant cleaner streets and hastened the departure of many vagrants and petty criminals. One lawyer of dubious reputation once protested this practice, declaring that his client was being forced into involuntary servitude and asked for a jury trial instead. "By a jury?" asked Judge Meyer. "What is dis jury?" The lawyer explained, "I insist that he be tried by his peers." Meyer exploded, "Oh, you do, do you? Well, I sentence him to two [additional] weeks on the chain gang, and I sentence you to one week for disrespect of the Court. Now, how do you like that trial by jury?"

Not all judges were as interested in justice as Meyer, however. Justice of the Peace James Burnett of Charleston held court wherever he happened to be, using a double-barreled shotgun as bailiff, keeping all fines he collected, and growing quite prosperous in the process. On one occasion Burnett pulled a drunken trail boss named Jack Harrer from the saddle, disarmed him, and on the spot fined him twenty head of three-year-old steers for disturbing the peace—steers which were placed on Burnett's ranch. When the County Board of Supervisors called on Burnett to report his fines, he replied that he kept no books and worked on a cash basis. The supervisors need not worry, he assured them, for his office was a self-supporting institution. Not until the 1890's did Burnett overstep himself. When a rancher upstream from his spread dammed the San Pedro River, Burnett dynamited the dam. In the flood of water that followed, the dam-builder's daughter drowned. The rancher shot Burnett without a word at their next meeting, and a jury acquitted him of murder in record time.

Just as judges in Arizona Territory varied in their capacities, so the peace officers ranged from excellent to poor. The first United States marshal, Milton B. Duffield, proved as adept at breaking the law as at upholding it. A legendary shot before his arrival in Arizona, Duffield came to the territory under a cloud of suspicion of fraud in California. In the territory he made a reputation for ferocity, bravery, and a willingness to shoot quickly. He soon grew tired of his scant salary and resigned. In 1871 he was brought to trial for assaulting the editor of the Tucson *Weekly Citizen,* but drew his pistol in court and walked out. He was killed in 1875 in a quarrel over ownership of a mine. In Navajo County, Sheriff Frank J. Wattron became notorious for his orders to his deputies not to bring in rustlers for trial but to shoot them on sight. Wattron also gained a reputation for his grisley sense of humor. It was his duty as sheriff to execute prisoners sentenced to hang in the county. In 1899 he sent invitations to the hanging of George Smiley, a railroad worker who had killed his foreman, that stated, "The latest improved methods of scientific strangulation will be employed and everything possible will be done to make the surroundings cheerful and the execution a success."

In contrast to such men as Duffield and Wattron were officers such as John H. Slaughter, the rancher who became sheriff of Cochise County at personal sacrifice and rid it of malefactors; Carl Hayden of Maricopa County, who as sheriff rarely carried a gun yet compiled an impressive record of arrests; Jeff Milton, federal customs collector for the territory who later declared, "I never killed a man that didn't need killing; I never shot an animal except for meat," yet who seriously discouraged smuggling across the border. Another peace officer of note was George Ruffner, sheriff of Yavapai County, who was noted for tracking down lawbreakers and bringing them in for trial.

From time to time the roily frontier conditions of Arizona brought together such a collection of criminals that normal law-enforcement procedures simply broke down. The discovery of precious metals, such as occurred at Tombstone in the late 1870's, attracted so many gamblers, fugitives, and gunmen that life and property became unsafe. Smuggling was rife, and rustling became practically a way of life. The gang headed by Ike and Billy Clanton moved their operations from Mexico to Tombstone, where they hoped to get rich from the big payrolls of the mines and the rich shipments of bullion. This brought the Clanton gang into conflict with the Earp brothers and their friend Doc Holliday. The sheriff at that time, John Behan, was a political appointee who could not stave off trouble, and it came on October 26, 1881—after fifteen seconds of shooting, generally labeled the "Gunfight at the OK Corral" but actually occurring in a nearby alley, Billy Clanton and two of his followers lay dead. The public sympathized with the Clantons, and several shots were fired from ambush at the Earps and their followers. Before the Earps could be brought to trial, they fled the territory to Colorado after shooting more of the Clanton gang, some in the back from ambush. The Earps were never extradited or made to pay for their crimes. On May 3, 1882, President Chester A. Arthur responded to the situation in Tombstone with a threat of marital law, but it was the election of John H. Slaughter to the sheriff's office that ended Tombstone's lawlessness, not the President's threat of martial law.

At times in Arizona, when inept or crooked judges and law officers gained the ascendancy or when local law-enforcement officials proved unable to maintain law and order, the citizens of the territory showed their desire for law and order by organizing local vigilante groups. In Tucson in 1873, for example, when a storekeeper and his wife were brutally murdered, a citizens' posse apprehended the murderers, gave them a public trial, and publicly executed all three, along with a condemned murderer

Tombstone Courthouse, today a State Park. *National Park Service*

The lynching of James Heith, the saloon-keeper who plotted the Bisbee Massacre. *Arizona Pioneers' Historical Society*

John H. Slaughter, the mild-mannered rancher who brought peace to Tombstone. *Arizona Pioneers' Historical Society*

A "zanjero" measuring water in an irrigation ditch near Tucson. *Arizona Pioneers' Historical Society*

Phoenix in 1891, the year of the great flood. *Arizona Pioneers' Historical Society*

President William H. Taft signing the Arizona statehood

George W. P. Hunt, seven times governor of Arizona. *Arizona Pioneers' Historical Society*

"Operation Haylift." The Air Force dropped hay to keep cattle alive during the great snowstorm of 1967. *United States Air Force, Luke Air Base*

awaiting execution. In 1879 residents of Phoenix broke into the jail, removed two men who had confessed to a murder, and executed them in public.

There was, on occasion, a curious blend of normal law-enforcement procedures with extralegal means. For example, in December of 1883 a gang robbed a Bisbee store filled with shoppers and fired indiscriminately into the crowd, killing three men and one woman. A posse quickly formed to track down the criminals. One member of that posse, a saloon-keeper named John Heath, so often tried to lead the posse on a false trail that the other members grew suspicious. Under questioning, Heath admitted that he had planned the robbery and named the actual perpetrators. The five actual robbers were arrested, brought to trial, and hanged; but Heath, who had not participated, was sentenced to twenty years in jail. This seemed a miscarriage of justice to the residents of Bisbee, who marched on the Tombstone jail, took Heath out to a nearby telegraph pole, and hanged him. A coroner's jury solemnly convened and, despite a photograph showing the dead man and the crowd around him, accepted the recommended findings of the coroner. Dr. George E. Goodfellow: "We the undersigned find that J. Heath came to his death from emphysema of the lungs—a disease common to high altitudes—which might have been caused by strangulation, self-inflicted or otherwise."

The growing demands of Arizona's citizens for law and order, for protection of person and property, along with the efforts of dedicated sheriffs, constables, Arizona Rangers, and federal officers gradually brought a more stable environment to the territory. Also aiding in the process was the Territorial Prison at Yuma—dubbed the "Hell Hole" by its inmates. This prison was authorized by the legislature in 1875 and opened the following year, built by convict labor. Prison discipline was harsh, but most of the prisoners were hard men. Conditions in most prisons of that day in the United States were severe, and several investigations found Yuma prison remarkably humane for that era. In 1909 the prison was moved to Florence, leaving the buildings to be converted into a high school. By the turn of the twentieth century, Arizona had become as peaceful as other states and territories, although it retained a reputation for violence that would provide subject matter for many imaginative writers.

The Passing of the Frontier

When the Territory of Arizona was created officially in 1863, it had no schools, no churches, no newspapers, no libraries, and no real cities. With the exception of the tiny settlements of Tucson and Yuma, along with a few ruins left at the site of abandoned mines, it had changed little from the time Coronado and other Spanish conquistadors first entered it. But between 1863, when the territory was created, and 1912, when it became a state, Arizona changed dramatically. In those short forty-nine years, it acquired the trappings of civilization, of culture, of polite society.

One of the first requisites of any civilized society is education. There were efforts to establish a school in Tucson as early as 1864 when, under the auspices of the Roman Catholics, a mission school was started at Mission San Xavier del Bac. It failed, however, just as did a Roman Catholic school in Tucson in 1866. Governor John N. Goodwin recognized the need of an educational system when he implored the First Legislature to enact a code establishing elementary, secondary, and university schools in the territory. That legislature responded by appropriating $250 apiece for schools in Tucson, Prescott, La Paz, and Mohave City—if each of those towns would match the sum. Only Prescott did so, and that by a special tax on gambling. Subsequent legislatures took ineffective steps to encourage education, but little progress was made. In 1870 in Tucson the Sisters of Saint Joseph of Carondolet opened an academy for girls and reopened a school for the Papago Indians at San Xavier.

Governor A. P. K. Safford in 1871 persuaded the Sixth Legislature to enact a broad school law for the territory, thereby earning for himself the title "Father of Arizona schools." With the passage of this law, which provided public funds, the city of Tucson opened a school for boys in March, 1871, taught by John A. Spring, an ex-soldier who had arrived in 1866. Other towns followed suit, and schools soon were available at most of them. Evidently most of the people agreed with Surveyor General John Wasson, who said, "We must either have schools or more jails, and we prefer the former."

Teaching at those pioneer schools was trying. Mary Elizabeth Post came to Arizona in 1872 to teach at Ehrenberg, traveling overland from San Diego to Yuma and thence by steamboat to her destination. She paused at Yuma to observe the efforts of Clara A. D. Skinner and Francis V. Bishop. "I visited the school," later wrote Miss Post, "so as to try to get something that would help me in my own work. There were pupils of all ages from married women to those just old enough to enter. . . . Only a very few knew any English, so the teachers just had to do the best they could. They taught the three 'R's' but you see how much they were handicapped. The school building on Main Street had formerly been the court house. It was of adobe and had three rooms—entrance hall, court room, and jail. The walls of the room that had been used for the jail was still covered with the scrawls of the prisoners, only white-washed over." Of her experience at Ehrenberg, she wrote, "My school room was a building formerly used as a saloon. . . . The floor was of earth. . . . Our furniture consisted of tables and chairs brought from the homes. I had fifteen pupils not one of whom knew any English; and I knew nothing of Spanish. . . . Sometimes an old prospector who had been used to visiting the saloon would wander in, and when he saw the new use to which his old stamping ground had been put he was more embarrassed than the young teacher and her pupils."

The first school in Bisbee was taught by Clara Stillman, who arrived from Bridgeport, Connecticut, in 1881. Her building was an unused miner's shack that had no doors, windows, or floor. For desks there were boards resting on packing boxes; seats were made by placing planks on nail kegs. Her own desk was a flour barrel turned upside down. There was no fire drill; "The Indian drill was the real thing," she later recalled. "Four blasts from the whistle at the hoisting works—two short, one long, one short— warned the villagers that there was danger, and women and little children as well as school boys and girls sought shelter in the [mine] tunnel."

Textbooks in those early schools were of every variety. Any book that could be found was used. Most school desks were so rough that pen and ink could not be used on them. Instead the students purchased slates, which sold for seventy-five cents and pencils at twenty-five cents. As there usually was no chalk for the blackboard (made of smooth boards nailed together and painted black), teachers improvised with talcum.

Gradually conditions improved as the legislatures in turn appropriated more and yet more funds. Half the money collected from gamblers' licenses went to finance education, while arrangements were made to hold "teachers' institutes" to upgrade the quality of education. Women were given the right to vote for school trustees. Then in 1881 came a uniform-textbook law. Finally, in 1885, the legislature provided for the establishment of a Normal School at Tempe (later to become Arizona State University), and in 1899 came Northern Arizona Normal School (now Northern Arizona University) at Flagstaff. Under such trying—if improving—conditions, education gradually became available to most children in Arizona at public expense.

The Territorial University came somewhat later. The legislature that created the first normal school also provided for the university. Dubbed the "Thieving Thirteenth," this legislature divided the spoils by giving Phoenix the Territorial Insane Asylum, Prescott the capital, Florence a bridge over the Gila River, and Tucson the University with an appropriation of $25,000. Tucsonans were so angry at not receiving the insane asylum, which carried an appropriation of $100,000, that they threw dead cats at their legislative delegation when it returned. Tucsonans were slow in organizing the University. Finally in 1891 it opened its doors to thirty-three students, most of whom were registered in the Preparatory School—actually a high school. There were so few secondary schools in the territory that the University had to provide this service.

Churches, as well as school buildings, were erected. Roman Catholic missionary work in Arizona had practically ceased during the Mexican era, and thus all Christian activity had come to a halt. Then in 1850, when the Territory of New Mexico had been created (which included Arizona), it had been made a vicariate apostolic (a missionary diocese) with Father John B. Lamy as its first bishop. He personally visited Arizona once, and once he sent a representative. Not until 1866 was he able to send a permanent padre to Tucson, Father J. B. Salpointe. Then on September 25, 1868, Arizona was organized as a separate vicariate apostolic with Salpointe as its bishop. Under his direction churches were built in most of the major cities, the Sisters of Saint Joseph of Carondelet were brought to start schools and hospitals, and various charitable works were conducted. In 1898 the vicariate was elevated to a regular diocese, with the title of Tucson. Some thirty years later the northern part of the state was separated and placed under the Diocese of Gallup. Many of the early bishops and priests were from France, although in more recent years residents of the state have filled the positions of the Roman Catholic church.

Protestant ministers doubtless crossed the territory bound for the California gold fields during the rush of forty-nine, but none stayed to establish churches. Next to arrive were members of the Church of Jesus Christ of Latter-day Saints (Mormons), who came in the 1850's; but they were recalled to Utah during the so-called Mormon War of 1857–58. They returned in the 1870's to establish communities in the White Mountains, such as Pinetop and Showlow; in central Arizona, such as Mesa and Lehi; in southern Arizona, on the outskirts of Tucson and at St. Davids; and in eastern Arizona at Safford and vicinity. To aid Mormons moving from Utah to Arizona, Jacob Hamblin established a "fort" at Pipe Springs (ten miles south of the Utah boundary in Mohave County) in 1858.

Then in 1870 Pipe Springs was permanently settled by a Mormon group headed by James M. Whitmore. In 1923 this symbol of Mormon determination became a National Monument.

The Colorado Conference of Methodists assigned the Reverend J. L. Dyer to Arizona in 1868, while Bishop O. W. Whitaker was appointed missionary bishop of Nevada and Arizona by the Episcopalians that same year. Baptists came soon afterward, along with representatives of other denominations. Some, such as the Dutch Reformed church, came especially to do missionary work among the Indians, but all contributed significantly to taming the frontier.

There was considerable growth of towns, even cities, during this same period. Tucson during territorial years was the largest. Established by Spaniards in 1776, it had some six hundred residents in 1846 when American troops first passed through. By 1871, when it was incorporated as a municipality by the legislature, it boasted three thousand citizens and was cosmopolitan in language, food, dress, amusements, holidays, ceremonials, and religious exercises. Believing that it was coming of age, the city in 1864 had passed an ordinance requiring that pigs be chained; no longer could they roam at large as they had previously. A windmill was erected in the Old Pueblo in 1873 by Hiram S. Stevens. About the same time L. C. Hughes planted grass and shade trees on his lawn, causing his neighbors to follow suit. Soon an ice plant was built, along with churches, schools, and a jail. The cavalry band from nearby Fort Lowell gave musical concerts, and J. S. Mansfield advertised the opening of a circulating library in 1873, the same year that a "Young Men's Literary Society" was announced.

Yuma came of age with the arrival of the railroad, although it had been a busy commercial center since steamboats began docking there in the early 1850's. Prescott was the site of the capital from 1864 to 1867 and from 1877 to 1889. Almost immediately after it was established, Prescott had saloons, stores, government offices, and a $5,000 theater. When mining in the vicinity declined, ranching increased in importance, and Prescott became a typical western ranching community.

Of all the cities in the territory, Phoenix proved the most surprising in its growth. It was founded in the late 1860's as a farming community to serve the Salt River Valley and had three hundred inhabitants by 1871 when it replaced its first name of Pumpkinville with the more prestigious Phoenix. A visitor in 1872 declared, "This is a smart town which had its first house completed about a year ago. Now it contains many houses; also stores, workshops, hotels, butcher shop, bakery, courthouse, jail, and an excellent school, which has been in operation for about four months. Lately hundreds of ornamental trees have been set out, which, in a few years, will give the town the appearance of a 'forest city' and will add to its beauty and comfort." Then in a prophetic vein, the visitor predicted, "When it has become the capital of the territory, which it will, undoubtedly, at no very distant day, and when the 'iron horse' steams through our country on the Texas and Pacific road, Salt River will be the garden of the Pacific slope, and Phoenix the most important inland town." The town was incorporated in 1881, by which time it had an ice plant. Citrus trees began producing six years later, providing an excellent commercial base for the community. That same year, 1887, a narrow-gauge streetcar line opened and the railroad arrived. With the moving of the capital there in 1889, the town boomed. Its growth is still astonishing.

Almost within weeks of the establishment of most towns in the territory, a newspaper would begin publication to predict an unlimited future for the community. The first newspaper, the *Weekly Arizonian*, began its career in Tubac in 1859, then moved to Tucson. It ceased to exist with the outbreak of the Civil War, but a paper entitled *The Arizonian* was issued in 1867 with the editorial statement: "When a few weeks ago we suspended publication of The Arizonian at Tucson we promised our friends and patrons that the paper would be reissued in Prescott about the first of September. The present issue shows that we have fulfilled that promise." Six years had elapsed. Prescott's first paper was *The Arizona Miner*, established by Secretary Richard C. McCormick and intended to further McCormick's political career. McCormick also financed the establishment in 1870 of the *Tucson Citizen*, which was edited by Surveyor General John Wasson. The *Citizen* was purchased by John Clum in 1877. Later it would become the *Tucson Daily Citizen*. Arizona's first daily newspaper was *The Bulletin*, established on March 1, 1877, by C. H. Tully. After four weeks it gave way to the *Tri-Weekly Star*. Later it was purchased by L. C. Hughes and in 1879 became the *Arizona Daily Star*. The first newspaper in Phoenix was the *Salt River Valley Herald*, a weekly that began in 1878. The following year it became the *Phoenix Herald*, and in 1899 it was consolidated with the Phoenix *Republican*, whose name later would be the illustrious *Arizona Republic*.

The growth of towns—and newspapers—was followed in short order by the establishment of libraries, musical societies, literary clubs, and sewing circles. All contributed to a current of intellectual activity, while the arrival of telegraph wires brought an awareness of national events and an end to narrow, parochial attitudes. Arizona easily entered the twentieth century along with the rest of the nation in 1901, for it had all the trappings of refined society. There was a growing awareness of this maturity, which brought a corresponding increase in demands for statehood and complete home rule.

THE QUEST FOR STATEHOOD

Until 1890, Arizonans were most concerned with internal matters, such as securing the railroad, developing their mineral wealth, establishing farms and ranches, and ending the Indian menace. During the 1880's, most of these goals became realities. Two transcontinental railroads were built, the renegade Indians were shipped to Florida, farms were laid out in the Salt River Valley, ranching spread to all parts of the territory, and the mineral wealth was exploited. By 1890, Arizonans knew relative security and could turn their thoughts to self-government and to the rising demand for statehood.

John Nichol Irwin was the first governor really to come face to face with this demand. A native of Iowa born in 1845, a graduate of Dartmouth, and a lawyer, Irwin had served as chief executive of Idaho from 1883 to 1885. On October 4, 1890, he was appointed governor of Arizona by President Benjamin Harrison. Irwin's major task as governor was to reunite the warring factions of the Republican party in Arizona, which had splintered badly under the brief and disastrous administration of Lewis Wolfley. The legislature in 1891 passed an act authorizing a constitutional convention, despite the fact that Congress had not enacted an enabling act. This convention, which met in Phoenix in September, consisted of seventeen Democrats and five Republicans. Its work was completed by October, and in December the constitution was endorsed by the voters of the territory (5,440 were for it, 2,280 against it). That constitution found strong opposition in Congress when it was submitted to that body, for it declared silver to be legal currency for the payment of state debts. The money issue was strong in national politics, with most congressmen believing that only gold should serve as currency. A bill to admit Arizona as a state, sponsored by Arizona's territorial delegate, Marcus A. Smith, a Democrat, easily passed the House of Representatives but died in the Senate. As the *Washington Post* stated, "The Times are not just now propitious for adding Democratic stars to the old flag." Republicans in the Senate feared the admission of a state that obviously would be Democratic in politics.

Irwin resigned as governor in April, 1892, to be replaced by Nathan Oakes Murphy, another son of Maine, born in 1849, who had practiced law and engaged in mining. Since 1889, Murphy had served as secretary of the territory, and he was a natural successor for Irwin. His term proved brief, however, for President Harrison failed to win reelection. When Grover Cleveland took the oath of office in March, 1893, Murphy—as was the custom—submitted his resignation. Just before going out of office, Murphy headed an unsuccessful delegation to Washington in an attempt to achieve statehood for Arizona. He continued to work to that end as territorial delegate to Congress, a position he held from March 4, 1895, to March 3, 1897.

Murphy's Democratic successor was Louis C. Hughes, publisher of the *Arizona Daily Star*, a Tucson newspaper.

Hughes was a Pennsylvanian who had come to Arizona in 1871 to regain the health he had lost during the Civil War. His wife, Josephine Brawley Hughes, was a fiery, strong-willed woman who dominated her husband and even set the editorial policies of his newspaper. An ardent temperance worker and militant feminist, Mrs. Hughes used her husband's position to further her causes. Hughes was unable to achieve statehood for Arizona despite the fact that both houses of Congress and the chief executive were Democrats. Reflecting his years in Arizona, Hughes stood for silver as legal tender, while the national Democratic party favored gold as the sole backing for currency. Hughes also quarreled with national leaders of his party over land policies in the territory. For these reasons he was unable to achieve statehood, and for the same reasons he was asked to resign in early 1896. He was replaced by Benjamin Joseph Franklin, a Kentuckian who served only a year. Franklin always claimed to be a descendant of the great American of the same name, but there is no evidence to confirm his claim. Franklin, who served in the Confederate Army under General Braxton Bragg, moved to Phoenix in 1892, where he practiced law until his appointment as governor. His term was too brief for any major accomplishments.

Governor Myron Hawley McCord was a political appointee, a man of poor record who reportedly became governor because as a congressman he had sat next to William McKinley, the President who in 1897 appointed him. Born in Pennsylvania in 1840, McCord had become a banker, newspaper publisher, and lumberman in Wisconsin, and had served one term in Congress. Moving to Arizona in 1893, he became a part owner of the Phoenix *Arizona Gazette*. He did little during his one-year term of office. When the Spanish-American War began, he resigned to become colonel of the First Regiment of Territorial Volunteers, a unit that never saw action and which was disbanded at the end of the war. McKinley then appointed him United States marshal for the territory.

Oakes Murphy, who replaced McCord, became the only territorial governor to serve two terms. Murphy pushed hard at the Republican National Convention of 1900 for a statehood plank for Arizona, and he secured it: "We favor home rule for, and the early admission to statehood of the Territories of New Mexico, Arizona, and Oklahoma," that document stated. And in 1901, President McKinley visited the territory, making vague promises of statehood. Disappointed citizens who met in Phoenix that year voted to establish a lobby in Washington to push their desires.

When Murphy retired from the governorship in 1902, President Theodore Roosevelt appointed an Arizonan, a friend from Rough Rider days in the late war, Colonel Alexander Osward Brodie. Brodie, a native New Yorker and a West Point graduate, had served under General George Crook in Arizona. He resigned his commission in 1877 and soon was ranching near Prescott and exercising his training as an engineer on the Walnut Grove Dam (which burst in 1891). He served as governor from 1902 to 1905, during which time there was some progress and great controversy on the statehood question.

The unexpected ascendancy of Theodore Roosevelt to the presidency, upon the assassination of William McKinley, revived statehood hopes in Arizona. Roosevelt had served in the Spanish-American War with the Rough Riders, an organization to which Arizona had contributed many soldiers. He should have been favorably inclined to the idea of the territory's desire for statehood. In addition, by the early 1900's, eastern capital had been heavily invested in Arizona's copper mines, and the monetary question had been resolved, removing still another source of opposition. A statehood bill was quickly introduced and seemed to be making satisfactory progress—when sudden opposition appeared from an unexpected source. Senator Albert J. Beveridge of Indiana, chairman of the powerful Senate Committee on Territories, introduced an amendment to the statehood bill calling for New Mexico and Arizona to be admitted as a single state. Republicans in the Senate feared that both New Mexico and Arizona would elect Democratic senators. With joint statehood, only two could be elected.

In pursuit of his joint-statehood quest, Senator Beveridge took his subcommittee on a tour of the Southwest. This group made a rapid jaunt through Arizona, spending only three days in the territory. Afterwards Beveridge announced that neither New Mexico nor Arizona had sufficient people alone to justify statehood, but that together they did. "Arizona is a mining camp," he declared, "and the bill admitting her is gerrymandered so shamefully that if the Republicans were to carry the State by 10,000, she would still send 2 Democratic senators to Washington." New Mexico, he asserted, was "in a much worse state educationally, and her senators would be dictated to by certain interests." His conclusion was foregone: the two territories did not deserve separate statehood, but did deserve statehood if they were admitted as a single state.

In April, 1904, a bill to that effect was introduced, calling for the capital of the joint state to be Santa Fe. Arizonans were horrified at the possibility, for at that time

New Mexico was an agricultural territory, which contained more residents than Arizona, residents who could be expected to vote high taxes on mines and low taxes on farms and ranches. Arizona's legislature in January, 1905, passed a resolution of protest to the bill which stated, "It threatens to fasten upon us a government that would be neither of, by, nor for the people of Arizona. It would be a government without the consent of the governed. . . . We . . . would rather remain forever a territory than to accept Statehood under such condition." This action of the legislature was warmly seconded by a convention held in Phoenix in May, 1905. That meeting resulted in the formation of the Anti–Joint Statehood League. Such opposition led certain congressmen to take a second look at the issue, and in October of that year another delegation visited the Southwest. Most of these visitors went away opposed to joint statehood.

In the midst of this stormy fight, Governor Brodie resigned. His replacement was the dignified Judge Joseph Henry Kibbey, best remembered for his famous decision— usually called the "Kibbey Decision"—that formed the basis of Arizona water law. Kibbey, born in Indiana in 1853, had moved to Arizona in 1888 to practice law at Florence. The following year he was appointed a justice of the Territorial Supreme Court, serving until 1893, after which he settled in Phoenix. Kibbey's appointment as governor was unusual in that he did not seek the office —it affords a prime example of the office seeking the man.

Kibbey was not able to aid the cause of statehood materially, for the fight had been transferred to Washington, where the struggle centered around Beveridge's joint-statehood bill. Beveridge pushed his bill with his oratory, declaring how mighty the single state which he called

Arizona would be: "Arizona, youngest of the Union and the fairest, how proud of her her citizens would be; how just a place she would hold in the nation's councils; not querulous, irritable and contentious, because of a consciousness of her scant population, but largeminded, generous and conciliatory, because of the knowledge of her greatness; not apologetic for her numbers, but serene in her popular equality with her associated states."

The debate over joint statehood was finally hushed by an amendment to the bill presented by Senator Joseph B. Foraker of Ohio, who favored separate statehood. The "Foraker Amendment" proposed that both New Mexico and Arizona should vote on joint statehood and that if either rejected it then joint statehood would be dead. Both houses of Congress accepted the compromise, and it passed. The election was held in November, 1906. New Mexicans accepted joint statehood by a vote of 26,195 in favor to 14,735 against. Arizonans rejected the proposal overwhelmingly, however, by a vote of 3,141 in favor to 16,265 against. Joint statehood was dead—but it seemed that statehood itself was dead also. Arizona had hardly moved from its position in 1890 when the agitation started —a territory.

In part because of the efforts of Governor Kibbey, the Republican party had a strong plank favoring statehood for Arizona in its platform of 1908. "We favor immediate admission of the Territories of New Mexico and Arizona as separate states in the Union," it asserted. Through the efforts of other Arizonans, the Democratic platform that year likewise advocated separate and immediate statehood for Arizona. President Roosevelt also urged the admission of Arizona upon Congress in 1908, but the measure was set aside until after the presidential election that year.

William Howard Taft, a Republican, was elected, and rumors soon were circulating that he favored statehood for the two territories. By this time, however, a new governor had been named for Arizona, Judge Richard Elihu Sloan. It was he who would guide the territory to statehood, who would be Arizona's chief executive when the long-desired goal was reached.

Part Three: **THE STATEHOOD YEARS**

A Valentine for Arizona

By 1909, Arizona had many factors working in favor of its petition for statehood. Its copper mines were producing an increasing stream of wealth; irrigated farming, along with ranching, showed tremendous promise; and eastern investments were high. Moreover, in 1908 the territory had elected a Republican delegate to Congress, Ralph H. Cameron. Arizona's production of wool, grain, and copper meant that its citizens possibly would favor a high tariff, which national Republicans were championing. In addition, the governor named by President Taft in

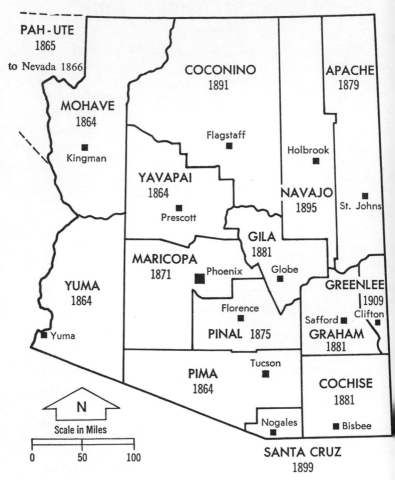

Arizona counties and county seats (with the date of creation of each county). *Drawn by Don Bufkin*

1909 was a man to inspire eastern confidence in the territory's ability to govern itself. Richard E. Sloan, born in Ohio in 1857, had graduated from Monmouth College in Illinois and worked as a journalist and prospector before graduating from Cincinnati Law School. In 1884 he moved to Phoenix, where he practiced law. From 1889 to 1893 he served on the Territorial Supreme Court, to which he was reappointed in 1897. There he remained until 1909—a man with a wide reputation for honesty and brilliance.

Yet just as the moment seemed propitious for securing statehood, new problems arose that placed the issue in doubt. In Arizona in 1909, organized labor was becoming a force, and leaders of this group were demanding liberal clauses in any proposed constitution. President Taft in his annual message to Congress in December, 1909, voiced his suspicion of radical elements when he suggested that an enabling act be passed for the two territories but urged the residents of the territories to exercise great caution in selecting delegates to their constitutional conventions. Congress responded by passing the enabling act in June, 1910, and Taft signed it. At last the territory seemed about to attain its goal.

Governor Sloan named September 12, 1910, as election day for the constitutional convention. The returns showed a Democratic landslide; they had won forty-one of the fifty-two seats. These delegates gathered in Phoenix and elected George Wiley Paul Hunt president of their body. Born in 1859, Hunt typified the rags-to-riches possibilities of Arizona. Arriving in the territory in 1881 a bankrupt prospector, this native of Missouri rose within ten years to the presidency of the Old Dominion Commercial Store and presidency of the bank. He became the first mayor of the town of Globe, then treasurer of Gila County. In 1892 he was elected to the lower chamber of the territorial legislature. Later he won three elections to the upper chamber of the legislature. Hunt boasted that he did not wear a "copper collar," meaning that he was no tool of the copper corporations. Such appeals enabled him to win the labor vote, and as an opponent of big business and a proponent of liberal legislation he dominated the constitutional convention.

The document that was produced definitely bore a "liberal" stamp. It provided for three branches of government; a governor with a two-year term and a low salary; a bicameral legislature, all legislators to serve only two years at a time; and popularly elected judges. Almost all officials were elected rather than appointed. Most controversial was the provision allowing the initiative, the referendum, and the recall. All public officials, including judges, were made subject to the recall. President Taft's opposition to the recall of judges and to other liberal provisions was so well known that the chaplain of the convention, the Reverend Seaborn Crutchfield, was moved to pray the morning following its adoption, "Lord, we hope that President Taft will not turn down the Constitution for a little thing like the initiative and the referendum. Lord, don't let him be so narrow and partisan as to refuse us self-government."

Their work concluded on December 9, 1910, the convention submitted the constitution to the voters of the territory. On February 9, 1911, it was approved by a vote of 12,187 to 3,302, and in August Congress passed a joint resolution admitting Arizona and New Mexico (where similar work had been done) as states in the Union. As had been widely predicted, President Taft vetoed the measure. He said the recall provision in the Arizona constitution threatened the independence and integrity of the judiciary. He stated his awareness that after statehood such a provision could be placed in the constitution and the federal government could not veto it, but as long as he could influence the matter, he intended to do so. Within a week, Congress passed another joint resolution excluding judges from the recall provision, and on August 21, 1911, Taft signed the measure. On December 12, 1911, the electorate of Arizona approved the deletion of the recall of judges from the constitution and elected a slate of public officials. George W. P. Hunt was elected governor, Sidney P. Osborn secretary of state, Marcus A. Smith and Henry F. Ashurst the United States senators, and Carl Hayden the representative in Congress. All were Democrats.

On the morning of February 14, 1912—Valentine's Day —a political struggle of half a century came to an end and a dream was realized when at ten o'clock President Taft signed the proclamation admitting Arizona to the Union as the forty-eighth state. Movie cameras recorded the event, the first time in history that a motion picture had been made of the President signing a law. In every city in the state there was wild celebrating as the telegraph brought news of Taft's signing of the act. Whistles shrieked at mines, factories, and power plants, schools were turned out so that children could participate in the parades; and almost every business closed. Governor-elect George Hunt led a parade up the street from the Ford Hotel, where he had spent the night, to the Capitol. He walked, he said, to illustrate the economy and simplicity of his administration. Joining him at the ceremonies was William Jennings Bryan, three-time Democratic nominee for President, who brushed aside questions about the possibility of his seeking a fourth nomination. Later in the day he made a two-hour speech. After the formal inauguration, Hunt returned to his hotel in the automobile which the legislature had already purchased for him. Thereafter Hunt regularly rode to work in the car, and, when questioned about his earlier pledge of economy, he would reply that he rode in order to get to his desk earlier.

The celebration following the inauguration was frantic. A forty-eight gun salute to the Baby State had to be halted after thirty-eight booming shots on account of the rattling of windows and panic among horses. Hunt appeared and made a short speech exuding optimism, after which there was singing, dancing, and general merrymaking. Statehood had come at last.

"I Promise If Elected . . . "

Arizona has produced few politicians as canny as George W. P. Hunt—and certainly none more colorful. As Arizona's first governor, six times re-elected to that position, he guided the state through its formative years, through labor crises associated with World War I, through the "Roaring Twenties," and through the first two years of the Great Depression. He did this despite a public "antibusiness" image, despite the creation of "100 clubs"—organizations of men who had contributed more than $100 to help defeat Hunt—and despite the efforts of members of his own party to turn him out of office. He maintained his position as the dominant force in Arizona politics by his own adroitness and by a careful attention to the wishes of the majority of voters. Hunt always publicly allied himself with the laboring class. He never spoke polished English, but he managed to make himself understood. Well-educated political opponents derided his pronunciation, his grammar, and his platform behavior—but it was Hunt who was elected.

Almost immediately after taking office in 1912, Hunt began working toward the election of 1914. He kept a file of names of the people he knew in each town and county. Periodically he visited all parts of the state, carrying these files with him. He usually traveled by automobile, and he would sit in the back seat studying his files as he went so that upon arrival he could call each person by name. On the return trip he jotted pertinent facts about the visit on the cards for use on the next visit. Hunt became extremely well known for his ability to call voters by name. His favorite causes as governor were good roads (he wanted paved roads constructed), an end to capital punishment, and prison reform. He joined two of these causes: good roads and prison reform. Since there was insufficient money in the state treasury to construct roads, Hunt used prisoners to build them. Convicts were sent to tent camps where gray uniforms replaced the traditional stripes, and they were set to work as road builders. The highway up Queen Creek between Superior and Miami constituted one such program; the highway between Tombstone and Bisbee another; and the bridge across the Salt River at Tempe a third. Labor unions and contractors opposed the governor's use of prisoners, but Hunt continued the practice.

Hunt was easily re-elected in 1914, defeating Republican Ralph H. Cameron. His second term was marred by labor disputes and strikes at Clifton-Morenci, where copper miners thought they were not receiving benefits commensurate with the rise in copper prices generated by

World War I. Hunt was forced to call out the National Guard, a move that cost him votes. As a result, the election of 1916 was hard fought and the narrowest in Arizona's history. Hunt's Republican opponent was Thomas Campbell, a native Arizonan, born in Prescott in 1878 and well known in Yavapai County politics. The first returns from the election of 1916 showed Campbell elected by 29,976 votes to 29,946 votes for Hunt, a difference of just 30 votes. Campbell was inaugurated on January 1, 1917. However, Hunt's forces demanded a recount by the Supreme Court. The results of this recount were announced on December 22, 1917, and showed Hunt had received 28,094 valid votes to Campbell's 28,051. Hunt was declared the winner by 43 votes. He was inaugurated on Christmas Day and received the whole year's pay.

As the election of 1918 approached, Hunt hinted privately to friends that he was not going to be a candidate for re-election, that instead he was going to wait for 1920 and contest the Senate seat held by Marcus A. Smith. Friends of Smith persuaded Woodrow Wilson to appoint Hunt minister plenipotentiary to Siam. Hunt accepted the position but spent his time in Siam writing post cards to every voter in the state; he had carried with him a list of all voters for that purpose. In 1922 he returned to the state more popular than ever, addicted to white linen suits and a pith helmet. These, along with his drooping mustache, brought him the nickname "Old Roman." He defeated Thomas Campbell by almost 7,000 votes in 1922 to return to the governorship. He won re-election in 1924 and 1926 before going down to defeat in 1928 to John Calhoun Phillips. Then came the depression of 1929, and the following year Democratic party leaders convinced the seventy-one-year-old Hunt to seek a seventh term. His political magic proved potent that year, and he defeated Phillips by twenty-five hundred votes. Unfortunately, his last term was marred by charges that he was using the newly created Highway Patrol as an instrument for political patronage. Hunt entered the Democratic primary in 1932 seeking an eighth term, but was defeated there by Dr. Benjamin Baker Moeur.

Hunt as governor served Arizona well. When he was first elected in 1912, the mood of the state was progressive, almost radical. Hunt bragged publicly about his anti-business stand, saying his front door was always open to the working class; what he did not advertise was that the back door was always open to businessmen. Just as Hunt realized the necessities of business, he knew that the democratic process worked by compromise, and he realized how important it was for him to thread a path for the state between the extremes of right and left. He was aware of the weakness of the constitution and shortly after taking office sought to change it by recommending amendments to the legislature. He knew that the governor of the state actually had very little power, either appointive or executive. Like his successors, he sought to gain more appointive power in order to make the state commissions and boards more responsive to him, just as he sought broader budgetary powers. These he failed to get, just as his successors have failed; but in the process of governing Arizona for fourteen years, Hunt left an indelible imprint on the state's government. He also left strong memories of himself with the voters; some hated him, some loved him, but none were indifferent to the "Old Roman."

Following Hunt was Thomas Campbell, the first Republican to govern the state. Campbell actually served most of the year 1917, only to be turned out when the

Supreme Court of the state declared that Hunt had won the election. Campbell then served under Herbert Hoover in the United States food administration and in the Treasury Department. In 1918, Campbell returned to Arizona, where he won the governorship by a scant 359 votes out of more than 51,000 cast. His margin in 1920 was almost 5,000 votes out of 67,000 cast. During Campbell's two administrations, the Nineteenth Amendment (women's suffrage) was ratified, a budgeting system for state expenditures was established, a water code for settling disputes was enacted, and a workmen's compensation law was passed (although later declared unconstitutional). Campbell was defeated by Hunt in 1922, however, and retired from the state political wars.

The only man ever to defeat George Hunt in a general election was John C. Phillips, a Republican born in Illinois in 1870. A lawyer, he moved to Phoenix in 1898 and worked as a carpenter's assistant during the construction of the state capitol building while studying to be admitted to the Arizona bar. Terms as a judge in Maricopa County and in the state legislature brought him to such prominence that in 1928 he was elected governor. During his term of office free county libraries were established, the state Bureau of Criminal Identification became a reality, and the Arizona Colorado River Commission was created. Because of the depression, Phillips, like most Republicans, lost in the election of 1930. George Hunt emerged from retirement to take the governorship from him.

Following Hunt's last term, Dr. Benjamin Baker Moeur became the state's chief executive by defeating Hunt in the Democratic primary of 1932 and then winning in the popular election. Moeur was born in Tennessee in 1869, graduated from Rush Medical College in Chicago, and then practiced medicine in Tombstone, Bisbee, and Tempe. Jokingly it was said he was elected by the adults he had delivered as babies. His major task as chief executive was contending with the depression, which he did by cutting the property taxes 40 per cent and instituting sales, luxury, income, and other taxes to make up the deficit. Also, the Twenty-first Amendment (repeal of prohibition) was ratified. The continued grip of the depression, however, caused voters to turn away from Dr. Moeur in 1936, after he had been re-elected two years before, and he was defeated in the Democratic primary after four years in office.

In 1936 the Democratic standard-bearer, and victor in the general election, was Rawghlie Clement Stanford, a native of Buffalo Gap, Texas. He had arrived in Arizona in 1881 at the age of two and lived near Phoenix. A checkered career as cowboy and soldier finally culminated in his admission to the Arizona bar in 1906. He became a judge in Maricopa County and served on a number of educational boards. His two years as governor were noted for passage of minimum wage laws, the outlawing of unfair sales practices, and the implementation of the federal Social Security Act in Arizona. Stanford chose not to seek a second term and retired to a private law practice. In 1943 he became a member of the Arizona Supreme Court, on which he served with distinction until 1955.

Stanford was succeeded as governor by yet another Democrat, Robert Taylor Jones. A native of Tennessee, Jones had a varied background that included his self-study of engineering, work on the railroad, a year as a construction worker on the Panama Canal, and an engineering job with a mining company in Nevada. He moved to Arizona in 1909, at the age of twenty-seven, to become an employee of various shortline railroads. Finally, he opened a drug store in Superior, expanding this to a chain of such establishments that made him prominent in the state and saw him elected to the legislature several times. In 1938, as a candidate, he urged a business administration of state government, and the voters liked what he said. He defeated Jerry W. Lee, the Republican, by almost fifty thousand votes. Unfortunately Jones's well-known friendship with certain members of the state senate hurt his effectiveness with members of the house. The legislature during his term did pass minimum wage legislation for public works employees, regulated the pardoning and paroling of convicts, and created the Arizona Department of Library and Archives. Jones chose not to run for re-election, retiring after one term in office.

His successor, also a Democrat, was the second native-born Arizonan to hold the post, Sidney Preston Osborn. Born in Phoenix in 1884, Osborn started early in Arizona politics. He was elected to the constitutional convention of 1910 at the age of twenty-four, the youngest member of that body; and, after statehood was achieved, he was elected to three terms as secretary of state. Afterward, he was associated with journalism, editing and publishing *Dunbar's Weekly,* a newspaper of political comment, from 1925 to 1940. Osborn was re-elected three times without serious opposition, becoming the first governor to serve four consecutive terms. His years in office were exciting ones for the state, the years of World War II and the postwar boom. Industry came to Arizona in a significant way during this period; huge military installations were constructed; the population almost doubled; social and educational needs were acute; and the underlying problem of water shortage had to be faced. Because the governor of Arizona had few powers under the constitution, Osborn had to rely on popular support to make the legislature move; he secured this support by appeals to the public over the radio. Osborn's greatest crisis came in September, 1945, when the Seventeenth Legislature met in special session to hear charges of impeachment against the governor. Osborn was charged with misuse of state funds in connection with the Colorado River dispute. The charge was quickly disproved and the governor's conduct and record were vindicated. Osborn died on May 25, 1948, while still in office, of amyotrophic lateral sclerosis, a form of paralysis that gradually deprived him of the use of his limbs and speech.

Arizona's constitution provides for no lieutenant governor. Thus, when Osborn died, the secretary of state, Dan E. Garvey, became the acting governor. A Mississippian, Garvey as a youth wanted to be a professional baseball player; instead, after various jobs, he became an accountant for the Alabama and Vicksburg Railroad. In 1909, at the age of twenty-three, he moved to Tucson to work for the Randolph Lines. Pima County politics qualified him to be appointed assistant secretary of state in 1938. When Harry M. Moore died in 1942, Governor Osborn appointed Garvey to be secretary; in 1944 and 1946 the voters endorsed the appointment by electing him to the office in his own right. On May 25, 1948, he became acting governor. That November, as Garvey was being elected governor, the voters of the state ratified a constitutional amendment establishing the line of succession to the governorship. Garvey was inaugurated as governor (not acting governor), a ceremony re-enacted on January 1, 1949. During his two years in office a Children's Colony was established, higher education received greater support, and a new highway code was enacted. Garvey, the fifth consecutive Democrat to hold office, was defeated in the primary in 1950 and retired from the office on January 1, 1951.

The election of 1950 saw the first feminine candidate for the governorship in Arizona's history; the Democrats nominated Ana Frohmiller, who had made a reputation for economy as state auditor. The Republicans responded by naming Howard Pyle, who had been born in Wyoming in 1906 and whose family had moved to Arizona in 1925. His background was in radio, where he had gained a wide reputation as the "Voice of Arizona." He won in 1950 by only 3,000 votes out of almost 200,000 cast, then was re-elected in 1952 by a wide majority. His administrations saw the Arizona Development Board, an organization formed to encourage industry to move to the state, come into being along with the establishment of legal districts for junior colleges. Perhaps the most important accomplishment of his administration, however, was the creation of the Underground Water Commission to prevent rampant pumping of that vital resource. Pyle sought re-election in 1954 but was defeated primarily because of his sending highway patrolmen to Short Creek, Arizona, where a small inoffensive sect of polygamists were discovered. Pyle's spectacular methods offended the sizable Mormon population of the state, who voted against him.

Ernest McFarland, an Oklahoman, was next to govern the state. After service in World War I, McFarland moved to Arizona but decided to complete his education with a law degree from Stanford University. He was admitted to the Arizona bar in 1920, at the age of twenty-six, and began practice in Pinal County, where he rose to become county attorney and a judge. In 1940 he was elected to the United States Senate, replacing Henry Fountain Ashurst. He served there until 1952 when he was defeated by Barry Goldwater. In 1954 he entered the race for governor and defeated Howard Pyle. During his four years in office, for he was re-elected in 1956, state aid to the public schools increased, a state parks system came into being, and work began on the interstate highway system. In 1958, McFarland chose not to run for a third time; instead he contested unsuccessfully to return to the Senate.

Arizona's fourth Republican governor since statehood, Paul Jones Fannin, was elected in 1958 and served three terms. Born in Kentucky in 1907, he was brought to Phoenix when just two months old. He completed his education at Stanford University, entered business in Phoenix and, became very successful. Later he and his brother formed a company for industrial development. Choosing the best men to aid him as governor, regardless of their political affiliations, Fannin worked tirelessly, especially to attract industry to the state. Further, he advocated the passage of legislation providing for a statewide tax equalization program, and he fought hard to secure more water for Arizona from the Colorado River. His hard work was rewarded by his election to the United States Senate in 1964.

In 1964, as an Arizonan was going down to defeat as a presidential candidate, Samuel Pearson Goddard, Jr., a Democrat, was winning the governorship. A loser in the gubernatorial race in 1962, Goddard carried the state despite a Republican victory in the fight for Arizona's presidential electoral vote. Born in Missouri in 1919, he was a graduate of Harvard and the University of Arizona Law School. His law firm in Tucson and his business interests prospered, while his interest in politics carried him into Democratic party work that led to his nomination in 1962 before his victory in 1964. His two years in office were marred by scandals in the Liquor Control Board, by the governor's paucity of real power under the constitution to lead effectively, and by political maneuvering within the Democratic party. In 1966 the voters rejected Goddard, as they did again in 1968.

Governing the state in 1971 was John Richard "Jack" Williams, who was born in Los Angeles in 1909. Moving to Arizona as a youth, he was a student at Phoenix (Junior) College before being employed by Key Investment Company, which owns radio stations in Phoenix and Tucson. Williams became a radio personality in Phoenix and throughout the state, gaining a popularity that enabled him to become mayor of Phoenix, the Republican gubernatorial nominee in 1966, and the winner in his bid for re-election in 1968. Court-ordered redistricting of the legislature in 1965 (in line with the "one-man, one-vote" ruling of the Supreme Court) saw the election in 1966 of a legislature in which both houses were dominated by the Republicans for the first time in Arizona's history. With Republicans in control of the legislature and the governor's office, the state government re-evaluated the tax structure of the state, increased state aid to education and the universities, and began work on the Central Arizona Project. Williams was re-elected in 1970 to serve the state's first four-year term, following a constitutional change.

Since statehood in 1912, there have been thirteen men elected governor: eight Democrats and five Republicans. Only two of the thirteen have been native Arizonans, reflecting the continuing influx of population and the paucity of natives. Most of these men have tried to streamline the constitution to allow more appointive power for the governor, consolidation of overlapping boards and commissions, more fiscal and budgetary powers for the chief executive, and fewer elective offices. Yet the people of the state have resisted such changes when these have been presented to them in the form of constitutional amendments, preferring to elect such officials as mine inspector, tax commissioner, and superintendent of public instruction. The governor, now as in 1912, still has very little real power except persuasion.

While there have been thirteen governors, there have been only eight United States senators. Both men elected to this office at statehood were Democrats, Marcus Aurelius Smith and Henry Fountain Ashurst. Smith, a lawyer from Tombstone, drew the short term in 1912, stood for re-election in 1914, and won. He was defeated in 1920 by Republican Ralph Henry Cameron. Cameron served only one term, losing in 1926 to Carl Trumbull Hayden, a Democrat. Hayden, the well-known sheriff of Maricopa County, already had served fourteen years as Arizona's sole member of the House when he was elected senator in 1926. Subsequently he was re-elected six times to the Senate, giving him seven terms in the House and seven in the Senate. When Hayden voluntarily retired in 1968, after a record forty-two years in the Senate, he was replaced by Republican Barry Goldwater.

The other line of succession to the United States Senate likewise has had four occupants. Henry Fountain Ashurst, a former cowboy and a lawyer, served until 1940 and gained a wide reputation as a "silver-tongued" orator. He was defeated in the Democratic primary in 1940 by Ernest William McFarland, who won re-election in 1948 and became majority leader of the Senate in 1952. Later that year, McFarland was defeated by Republican Barry Morris Goldwater in one of the great political upsets of Arizona history. Goldwater, a native Arizonan, quickly moved into national prominence as a senator, for he became the leader of the conservative forces in the country. This prominence brought him re-election in 1958 and the Republican nomination for president in 1964. Goldwater was defeated in his bid for the presidency, and his Senate seat was won by outgoing Governor Paul Jones Fannin. Four years later, in 1968, Goldwater won the seat vacated by Carl Hayden and returned to Washington.

Arizona has had only eleven congressmen representing its interests in Washington. Carl Hayden, the state's lone representative for seven terms, was succeeded by Lewis William Douglas, of the mining family, who served until his resignation in 1933. Douglas was succeeded by Isabella Selmes Greenway, the widow of John C. Greenway and owner of copper mines at Ajo. Mrs. Greenway served until 1936, when she was replaced by John Robert Murdock, a professor of history and government in Arizona State Teachers College at Tempe, who won eight consecutive terms before going down to defeat in 1952. In 1940, Arizona gained a second seat in Congress, which was won in 1942 by Richard Fielding Harless, a Maricopa County attorney. When he chose to run, unsuccessfully, for governor after three terms, his seat was filled by Harold Ambrose Patten, an outstanding football player at the University of Arizona, where he later served as a football coach. Patten also served three terms. Arizona's first Republican representative was John Jacob Rhodes, who in 1952 defeated Professor Murdock. Rhodes, an attorney, has won re-election since and was still serving in 1971. Congressman Patten did not run for re-election in 1954;

his seat was won by Democrat Stewart Lee Udall, member of a prominent Arizona Mormon family and a lawyer. Udall resigned in 1961 to become secretary of the interior in the Kennedy administration, a position he held under President Lyndon Johnson as well. His seat was won by his younger brother, Morris King Udall, also a lawyer, who still held the position in 1971 through subsequent re-elections. Arizona's third seat, gained after the census of 1960, was apportioned to the northern part of the state. First to occupy the position was George Frederick Senner, Jr., a Democrat from Miami, who was re-elected in 1964. Senner lost in 1966 to colorful Sam Steiger of Prescott; Steiger won re-election in 1968 despite heavy and well-financed opposition, as he did in 1970.

At the local level Arizona is divided into fourteen counties, each administered by a board of three commissioners elected for four-year terms. Under the provisions of the constitution, there are no restrictions on the re-election of officials, but all, including judges, are subject to recall. The legislature currently is composed of a thirty-member Senate and an eighty-member House of Representatives. Members of both houses serve two-year terms and meet in annual session. Five state supreme court justices serve staggered six-year terms. There is at least one superior, or county, court in each of the fourteen counties, with such populous counties as Maricopa (Phoenix) and Pima (Tucson) having several courts. All judicial officials are popularly elected. Citizenship in the state is earned through a one-year residence. A citizen must have resided in his county and precinct at least one month in order to vote.

Arizona's politics have been colorful, if not efficient. For years journalists referred to the state's "Cowboy Legislature," meaning that it was dominated by ranching and farming interests, but court-ordered redistricting in 1965 gave 50 per cent of the seats in both houses to residents of Maricopa County and another 20 per cent to Pima County. As a result, the legislature now is dominated by urban elements. Another striking change is the shift to the Republican party. For the first forty years following statehood, almost all offices were held by Democrats. In 1971 both senators, two of three congressmen, the governor, and a majority of both houses of the legislature were Republican, despite the fact that the Democrats held a commanding majority of registered voters. The future of politics in Arizona is uncertain, promising only to continue to be colorful.

THE MINERAL FRONTIER EXPANDS

For buyers of shares of stock in Arizona's mining corporations, it was the ugly duckling that became a beautiful swan. Shares of stock in copper companies that originally sold for 50¢ rose to $50. The mining of this resource did not begin on a large scale until about 1875, although copper had been mined at Ajo as early as 1854. At that time the ore was shipped all the way to Wales for smelting and still showed a profit. Pioneers of the 1850's, 1860's, and early 1870's thought so little of copper that when, in their prospecting, they found deposits of the mineral, they disregarded them. Emerson Oliver Stratton, for example, was at Ajo in 1875 but commented later, "There was no profit in copper at the time and we did not hold it [the mine]." The Ajo deposit passed through several owners until 1912 when it was acquired by John Campbell Greenway, who made a fortune from his New Cornelia Copper

Company. In 1938 the mine was valued at $18,000,000, and it is still being operated profitably.

Copper became valuable because of the electrical revolution and because rail transportation became available. The ratio of price to poundage made cheap transportation a necessity. The arrival of the railroad, coincidental with the growing needs of the electrical revolution, the telephone, and the telegraph, prompted prospectors to begin an avid search for what they once had been disgusted to find. Several areas would emerge as rich in this mineral: in east-central Arizona near Clifton-Morenci; in southeastern Arizona at Bisbee-Douglas; in central Arizona at Globe-Miami-Ray-Superior; in northern Arizona at Jerome; in southwestern Arizona at Ajo; and in south-central Arizona in the vicinity of Tucson.

The first successful copper mining in modern Arizona was conducted by the Metcalf brothers, Jim and Bob. On a scouting expedition against Apaches they discovered copper croppings in 1870, and they began development of their Longfellow and Metcalf mines about 1872. The ore was so rich that it was "quarried rather than mined," according to one report. In 1873 a smelter was constructed at the site, near the present Clifton-Morenci, the first copper smelter in the Southwest. By 1882 the Metcalf-Clifton-Morenci mines had produced twenty million pounds of copper, a shortline railroad had been constructed to Lordsburg to transport the output, and the Arizona Copper Company had paid rich dividends. In 1912 the company was purchased by the Phelps Dodge Corporation, an emerging giant of the copper industry.

The Bisbee mines were discovered in 1875. A claim named the Copper Queen was located by Hugh Jones, but he thought so little of it that he allowed his title to lapse. George Warren relocated the claim, but he had little confidence in it. He bet his ownership on a foot race and lost, making this one of the most expensive races in history—his shares eventually were worth an estimated $13,000,000. The mine later was sold to James Reilly for $28,000, who in turn sold it to a group of purchasers for $1,250,000; that group organized the Copper Queen Mining Company, and sent Dr. James Douglas, a physician turned geologist, to manage the works. The town of Bisbee grew in the vicinity, a rough town that could match Tombstone in violence. When the smelter fumes killed most plants in the vicinity, it was moved east to a town named Douglas. Gradually, the Copper Queen came to dominate copper mining in southeastern and east-central Arizona. In addition, it bought up the mines at Tombstone as flooding occurred some one thousand feet below ground level and halted silver mining there.

The first mine at Globe was located in 1873, but production did not get underway until 1878. By 1884 the mine was yielding three thousand tons of ore a month, while the smelter produced 7.4 million pounds of copper that year. In 1904 the company was reorganized as the Old Dominion Company. Under skilled management and improvements of $2,000,000, the mine yielded handsome profits. At nearby Superior, the Magma Copper Company acquired title to the Silver King mine, which had ceased to produce significant amounts of silver, and found rich copper ore. Miami mushroomed in 1907 because of real estate promoters, but the development of the Miami Copper Company and the Inspiration Copper Company produced a solid foundation for the town. During World War I, the prices of copper soared, and a large smelter was constructed, providing jobs for residents. The Ray Copper Company, organized in 1884 at the town of the same name by two Tucson merchants, Albert Steinfeld and Louis Zeckendorf, paid few dividends until 1906. In 1933 it was acquired by the Kennecott Copper Corporation and has been a steady producer and large employer of Arizonans. The Silver Queen mine was located near the old Silver King mine but had failed to produce the precious metal. This property was acquired in 1910 by the Magma Copper Company; the shafts were deepened; a smelter was erected; and copper was produced in handsome quantities. Today it is one of the few copper companies in Arizona to mine by tunneling, as opposed to the open-pit method usually associated with copper.

The United Verde Company at Jerome-Clarksdale illustrates the spectacular rise in value of shares in a copper company. Originally located in 1880 and worked for precious metals, it was abandoned in 1885 and stock in the company declined rapidly in value. Then, in 1888, William Andrews Clark of Montana grew interested in the property. Clark, a self-made millionaire many times over, had developed the Anaconda holdings at Butte. When he arrived in Arizona in 1888, he insisted on a personal inspection of the United Verde. Clad in overalls and carrying a rock hammer, he spent three weeks exploring the mine, then bought a majority of the stock in the company that owned it. In a short time it was producing five million pounds of copper a month. Since 1900 it has paid $72,000,000 in dividends and has played Santa Claus to those Arizonans who held shares in it. After World War II the mine ceased production, and now the town of Jerome is the site of a state park.

Between 1870 and 1910, the years when copper was

desperately needed for the electrical revolution, Arizona's copper-producing mines were developed. Then came World War I, a conflict that boomed the price of copper. In 1914 the price averaged 13.6 cents a pound; by 1916 it had risen to 27.2 cents a pound, exactly double what it had been only two years before. Production naturally rose. In 1915 the state produced 432 million pounds, while in 1920 it produced 559 million pounds. By 1926 the figure had risen to 723 million pounds. The prosperity was for stockholders, however, not for the miners. Their wages did not increase as the price of copper advanced. Thus there was severe discontent among Arizona's miners during World War I. Union organizers and radicals came to the state to capitalize on this discontent.

In the Clifton-Morenci-Metcalf area, the first strike occurred in 1915. The workers—angry at their low wages, the company's high profits, the cost of company housing, and the prices of goods and services at the company stores and hospitals—invited the Western Federation of Miners into their district to organize a union. The Western Federation of Miners was a radical organization which believed in "direct action" to achieve its ends. By September 12 the strike was effective at all three towns, and violence seemed imminent. Governor Hunt responded by sending in members of the state guard. Fires destroyed part of the conveyor system at Clifton—part of the "direct action" advocated by the Western Federation of Miners. But company officials could afford to outwait the miners. By January, 1916, the men were living on relief funds and agreed to return to work while negotiations took place. A settlement was reached, but it was inconclusive. In the next year and a half there were seventeen more strikes, mostly minor in character until July 1, 1917, when another major strike occurred. This time the owners closed the mines to starve out the strikers, but owing to the war, a presidential commission came from Washington and negotiated a settlement.

Similar discontent at Bisbee produced a major strike in July, 1917. The organizers of this strike were members of the Industrial Workers of the World, an organization which opposed American participation in the war. Therefore the leaders of the strike could be branded as unpatriotic (and unwanted) nonresidents. Citizens of Bisbee decided to deal forcibly with them and with their followers to end the strike which had idled 15,000 miners. On the night of July 11–12, Sheriff Harry C. Wheeler and a posse of 1,200 armed citizens rounded up labor leaders, vagrants, and other undesirables. These 1,286 people were loaded on a train, moved eastward, and forced out on the desert near Hermanas, New Mexico. The "Bisbee Deportation," as this action was called, broke the strike, and the miners returned to work.

By the early twentieth century, copper had produced far more wealth for Arizona than its gold and silver mines combined. Nevertheless, some precious metals are still being produced in the state, usually as a by-product of copper mining. Gold and silver frequently are found in conjunction with copper, but in minute quantities. Advanced methods of refining the copper, such as now are used, extract every ounce of gold and silver. For example, in 1950 Arizona produced some $130,000,000 in copper as well as $4,000,000 in gold and $4,000,000 in silver. That same year the state also produced $15,000,000 in zinc and $10,000,000 in lead.

The recent instability in Latin-American governments and their nationalistic tendencies to expropriate American-owned property, along with the continued demands of the electronics age, has brought a resurgence of activity to copper mining in Arizona within the past decade. For example, Pima County in 1954 had only one producing mine, the New Cornelia at Ajo, by then a subsidiary of Phelps Dodge. Then the American Smelting and Refining Company developed a mine at Silver Bell (some forty miles northwest of Tucson) at the same time that the Banner Mining Company was reactivating its properties near Twin Buttes (about twenty miles southwest of Tucson). Adjacent to that site, the Pima Mining Company opened another deposit and began production. By the mid–1960's Pima County was producing 15 per cent of the nation's copper. The rest of the state was producing 37 per cent, bringing Arizona's production to 52 per cent of the national total. In 1966 alone, mining activity in Arizona was valued at approximately $610,000,000 and was the second largest factor in the state's economy.

Today the mining industry, principally copper, pays a large share of the state's taxes, employs more than five per cent of the total workers, and accounts in large measure for the state's growth and prosperity. Labor relations are still stormy, however, and the workers still believe that they are not sharing equally in the prosperity. Long and costly strikes, such as the eight months' deadlock of 1967, have produced bitterness and hatred, even violence on occasion. To avoid such problems, the copper companies are trying to rid themselves of the company-town, company-store, company-hospital image. They are selling properties linked to this image and encouraging private industry to take over such functions. Yet, despite such labor disputes the history of labor relations in the copper and mining industries of Arizona compare favorably with those of the steel industry, the automotive industry, and other national industries. While there has been bitterness in the past, Arizona as a whole can be proud of its mineral industry, which continues to be a bonanza for the state's economy.

THE COLORADO RIVER CONTROVERSY

Arizona's water problem since statehood has been the same twofold problem it was during territorial years and even before that—for ten to eleven months a year too little water and during the remaining one or two months too much water. The rain that falls in the state is not spread evenly. For most of the year there are only traces, and then come downpours that flood arroyos and river valleys, giving meaning to road signs warning, "Danger in flood season." Arizonans have built dams for flood control as well as for irrigation and for the concomitant benefit of hydroelectric power. The success of Roosevelt Dam, completed just before statehood, pioneered the building of such dams and proved the feasibility of such projects. Even before federal financing for additional projects became available, several more dams were constructed, principally in the Salt and Verde river valleys. In 1925, Horse Mesa Dam, the second such project, was completed below Roosevelt Dam, forming Apache Lake. Mormon Flat Dam (Canyon Lake) and Stewart Mountain Dam (Saguaro Lake), along with Roosevelt and Horse Mesa dams, brought the Salt River under control. The Verde was tamed by the construction of Bartlett and Horseshoe dams, while a seventh dam was constructed on Cave Creek (north of Phoenix).

But Arizonans, in their quest for water to store behind such dams, quickly learned that their neighboring states also were searching and fighting for water, and that a dam built in one state more than likely trapped water that fell as rain in another state. Most of the rivers worth damming crossed state lines, making co-operative efforts necessary in order for all states to get a fair share of what little water was available. The principal river of the Southwest was the Colorado, which drained 95 per cent of Arizona. By 1920 Westerners called it "The West's last great water hole." The seven states drained by the Colorado agreed to a conference to discuss the damming and distribution of Colorado River water. Congress in 1921 approved the meeting and authorized a commission, composed of one representative from each of the seven basin states plus a federal commissioner, to meet in Santa Fe in November, 1922.

While this meeting was in progress, Governor-elect George Hunt publicly stated his position. He said that Arizona would accept no program for developing the Colorado which compromised the state's rights. He asserted that water from the Colorado should not be used in Mexico (despite a Mexican rightful claim under the rule of prior appropriation), that California would try to usurp water properly belonging to Arizona, and that the program should be undertaken over several years only as money became available. The federal delegate to the Santa Fe meeting, Secretary of Commerce Herbert Hoover, immediately invited Hunt to sit with the group in Santa Fe, hoping to forestall opposition. Hunt declined.

On November 24, 1922, the meeting in Santa Fe concluded with the signing, by all seven states, of the Colorado River Compact, which projected the development and utilization of the water from the Colorado. Half the water, an estimated total of fifteen million acre-feet, would go to the Upper Basin states of Utah, New Mexico, Colorado, and Wyoming, and the other half to the Lower Basin states of Nevada, California, and Arizona. California was to get 4,400,000 acre-feet, Arizona 2,800,000, and Nevada 300,000. The Arizona delegate to this convention signed the compact, and Governor Campbell urged ratification of it. But Hunt, who was inaugurated on January 1, 1923, opposed it so effectively that the legislature refused to ratify it. Thus Arizona alone, of the seven basin states, refused to sign. And Arizona's Congressional delegation bitterly opposed passage of the Swing-Johnson Act, signed by Calvin Coolidge on December 21, 1928, which authorized the building of Boulder Dam on the Colorado; water trapped behind it would be allotted under the Colorado River Compact. Arizona next contested the act in the courts, arguing before the United States Supreme Court that the construction of such a dam within Arizona's borders required the consent of the state engineer and that such consent had not been given. The Supreme Court rejected the Arizona argument, ruling that under the Constitution Congress had authority over navigable streams. Thus the Swing-Johnson Act was legal.

President Herbert Hoover proclaimed the Boulder Canyon Project Act in effect in 1930. This dam would provide water to irrigate some one million acres in both Arizona and California. Nevada and Arizona each would receive 18 per cent of the electric power generated; and the All-American Canal was to be constructed to distribute the water. Elwood Mead, United States commissioner of reclamation, superintended the construction of the dam, which was completed on March 1, 1936. Lake Mead, a 115-mile reservoir, could hold thirty-one million acre-feet of water behind what eventually was named Hoover Dam.

Arizona again went to court, this time to prevent California from getting a lion's share of the water. In this action Arizona argued that it should receive an additional one million acre-feet of water to compensate it for inclusion of the Gila River within the compact. The court again rejected Arizona's arguments, stating that the state could not assert a claim to water under the Colorado River Compact since it had not ratified the compact: "If Arizona's rights are in doubt," asserted the court, "it is, in large part, because she has not entered into the Colorado River Compact."

The federal government proceeded with building other dams on the Colorado even before Hoover Dam was completed. Twenty miles upstream from Yuma, Imperial Dam and reservoir were constructed, just above Laguna Dam, completed in 1907 to raise the water level for purposes of irrigation. Water impounded by Imperial Dam is used in the Wellton-Mohawk Project east of Yuma in the Gila River Valley and in the Imperial Valley of California. In 1934 the government began constructing Parker Dam, between Hoover and Imperial dams, to supply water to Los Angeles. Governor Benjamin B. Moeur believed that desperate measures were necessary to prevent the loss of this water to Arizona. He called out the National Guard and sent it to the site of Parker Dam to halt work. On January 14, 1935, the federal government went to court seeking an injunction against the state so that work could continue. In the case *United States v. Arizona*, however, the Supreme Court announced in April, 1935, that Arizona was right—there was no statutory authorization for the construction of Parker Dam. Congress soon passed legislation specifically authorizing the construction of Parker Dam, and Governor Moeur was forced to give way.

The troops were withdrawn, construction was started, and Parker Dam was completed in 1941. It impounds Lake Havasu and supplies water to the coast by means of the Los Angeles Aqueduct.

In 1936, Arizona went to court yet a third time, seeking the apportionment of the unappropriated waters of the Colorado on an equitable basis and asking that California's share of such water be limited. Arizona's suit was dismissed, however, for the federal government had not agreed to be sued. This left the state with no recourse but to ratify the Colorado River Compact. This it did in special session of the legislature in 1944—when industrialization during the war years created a severe water and power shortage. The state negotiated a contract with the secretary of the interior for the delivery of 2.8 million acre-feet of water to Arizona from the Colorado River.

Meanwhile other dams either were constructed or at least planned. In the early 1960's a flood-control dam was completed at Painted Rocks near Gila Bend. Another was erected on the Bill Williams River, while the Carl Pleasant Dam was constructed on the Agua Fria. A dam equal in scope to Hoover Dam has now been completed on the Colorado, Glen Canyon Dam, which impounds Lake Powell, estimated when full to be two hundred miles long.

The most grandiose project to satisfy Arizona's water needs was conceived by Fred T. Colter, who proposed the pumping of water from the Colorado River through tunnels in the mountains so that the water would flow into the central river basins of the state. Originally known as the Highland Project, it has been relabeled the Central Arizona Project. This plan drew the support of the Arizona Interstate Stream Commission, a nonpartisan state board created to secure water for Arizona; the Central

Arizona Project Association, a voluntary citizens' group; and the United States Bureau of Reclamation, which declared the project feasible. All major newspapers in Arizona voiced their support, as did most private citizens, with the exception of residents living in the vicinity of Parker and Yuma, who feared the Central Arizona Project would deprive them of water already being used for irrigation.

With this plan in mind, Arizona's congressmen began fighting for federal authorization and funding. Likewise the state attorney general began fighting to make certain that enough water would be available from the Colorado to make the project workable. The major contestant for water was California, and in 1953 California made diversions from the Colorado in excess of the 4.4 million acre-feet it had previously agreed would be its maximum diversion. Arizona brought suit against California for an excessive diversion. The case of *Arizona v. California* came to trial on June 14, 1956. After 22,593 pages of testimony, 4,000 exhibits, and advice and opinions from 105 technical and scientific experts, Judge Simon Rifkind reached a decision in what he called "the greatest struggle over water rights in the latter-day history of the West." His decision was a victory for Arizona. California was limited to 4.4 million acre-feet of water annually, Arizona was to get 2.8 million acre-feet, and any surplus over the allotted amount would be divided equally between Arizona and California. This meant that water was available for the Central Arizona Project, some one million acre-feet annually. Subsequently, in 1963, the Supreme Court upheld Judge Rifkind's findings, stating specifically that the waters of the Gila River were reserved to Arizona and were not to be counted as part of the Colorado River's drainage.

After a long and difficult fight, Congress finally approved the Central Arizona Project in 1968. Funding followed which allowed work to begin. By 1972, when this project will be completed, the acreage under irrigated cultivation should increase dramatically in the state. Also, water to meet the needs of a growing Phoenix and Tucson should be available, relieving these cities' dependence on other sources of water. This increase in the supply of water will be especially appreciated by farmers, who have complained that wells pumping underground water up for urban consumption are lowering the water table and harming those engaged in agriculture.

Just before World War II, the pumping—some call it "mining"—of underground water began on a large scale to irrigate crops. Driven by diesel or electric motors, the pumps by the 1950's were supplying water to half the irrigated acreage in the state. The problem was the drastic lowering of the water table that followed. Wells that originally pumped at a fifty-foot depth had to be lowered and then lowered again, and early users began demanding protection under the law of prior appropriation. During the 1950's the legislature sought a satisfactory solution by restricting further reclamation of desert land and by declaring certain areas of the state to be critical water areas—meaning that no more wells could be drilled in these areas. Even with this legislation, the water table has continued to drop in most parts of the state. Farmers had to drill deeper and deeper, while cotton prices fell, with the result that bankruptcy followed for many of them.

The fight for water still goes on. Many citizens of the

state are hoping that the Central Arizona Project will solve the water problems of Arizona. However, the rapid growth of population, the expanding needs of industry, and the explosion of urban consumers project more water crises in the future. Perhaps not until ocean water can be desalted cheaply and pumped into the state will there be a permanent solution. Water is still needed for the thirsty land.

NEW BONANZAS

Statehood—so long anticipated—brought much satisfaction and many problems. Responsibility accompanied self-government in ways unanticipated on Valentine's Day, 1912. Good political leaders had to be selected by the voters; water for Arizona's growing needs had to be secured; provision had to be made for a rapidly expanding population; education had to be financed; tax monies had to be raised to underwrite the cost of myriad state services. Arizonans proved resourceful in coping with the problems and responsibilities of statehood and self-government, and rapid progress was made.

In 1912, when Arizona became a state, the only real source of transportation for goods and people was the railroad. Many residents of the state were concerned with the paucity of good roads. With the development of the automobile, paved highways became more and more a necessity and less and less a plaything of the rich. Arizonans in significant numbers joined enthusiastically in the "good roads" movement. As many residents of the state liked to spend the hot summer in California, the first move was to secure ready transportation to the West Coast. Joining with the Automobile Club of Southern California, Arizonans promoted the building of highways by the Cactus Derby, an overland road race from Los Angeles to Phoenix. The finish of this annual race at Phoenix marked the high point of the state fair. The first race was held in 1908, as a compromise between sportsmen members of the club, who saw the automobile as a sporting medium, and the utilitarians, who realized the growing usefulness of it. The final Cactus Derby was held in 1917; after World War I brought the contest to an end, it was not reactivated. The course of the race varied; some years it ran from Los Angeles to San Diego, Yuma, and Phoenix, while in other years it went from Los Angeles to Needles, Prescott, and Phoenix. Both routes had tortuous terrain that tested men and cars to the limits of endurance, but year after year the most famous names in automobile racing entered it—men such as Barney Oldfield, Louis Chevrolet, Olin Davis, and Louis Nikrent—to win a medal bearing the inscription "Master Driver of the World."

Such publicity for the "good roads" movement did have effect. Spanning the desert dunes west of Yuma, a plank road was built, allowing easy transit. Opened shortly after statehood, this road served until the 1930's, and traces of it can still be seen along the present interstate highway. With passage on July 11, 1916, of the Federal-Aid Road Act, more funds became available for construction, but not nearly enough for so large a state as Arizona and one containing so few people. Despite Governor Hunt's use of convict labor, progress was painfully slow. By 1929, Arizona had only 281 miles of paved roads. During the 1930's, as an antidepression measure, more funds for construction were made available, and much progress was made. Yet the tax base in Arizona was simply too small to finance large-scale construction. In 1944, Congress passed the

Federal Highway Act establishing a national system of interstate highways, and funds from this source allowed the completion of U.S. Route 66 and U.S. Route 80, the two major arteries across the state from east to west. Then, in 1956, the Interstate Defense System was created by Congress, providing 90 per cent federal payment for multiple-lane, controlled-access roads. This system is now virtually complete in Arizona, allowing rapid transportation to most areas of the state. The "good roads" movement has seen its goals largely fulfilled.

The first airplane to disturb the Arizona skies soared over Phoenix in 1908. Three years later, in a national coast-to-coast race for a large prize, aviators crossed the state from east to west and from west to east; one aviator set a world's record on that flight by going the 165 miles from Yuma to Maricopa in 206 minutes. At the Pima County Fair in 1915, air mail service was provided from the fairgrounds to the downtown post office, and in 1917 Tucson established the first municipal airport in America. Reflecting the giant strides made in aviation during World War I, the Arizona Aviation Company in 1920 tried to establish commercial service in the state. Although the attempt failed, it demonstrated the possibilities of aviation in Arizona. Seven years later the Aero Corporation (later called Standard Airlines) began service from Los Angeles to Phoenix and Tucson. By 1930 there were eighteen airports in the state. Then came World War II, which provided an even stronger impetus to flying than World War I. After that conflict, commercial aviation was serving all major cities in the state. Today, with crop dusters aiding farmers in all parts of Arizona, every town, along with many farms and ranches, has an airstrip, while the cities are major hubs of aviation activity. Also, a number of Air Force bases are located in the state.

During those first years of statehood, foreign events were of major importance to Arizona. Across the international boundary in Mexico, revolution followed revolution, with rebel forces fighting the national troops of that Republic at Nogales and Agua Prieta (both in Sonora). To prevent incursions on American soil, National Guard units and regular army troops were stationed along the border. Then, just five short years after statehood, came World War I. At first many Arizonans feared that involvement in this conflict would cause unemployment and economic stagnation. Just the opposite occurred. Copper prices doubled, bringing rapid expansion and growth to mining in the state. The need of cloth for uniforms increased the price of cotton, and farmers hastily plowed and planted this staple; in fact, so much grazing land in the state was converted to cotton during the conflict that the dairy industry suffered. Ranchers profited also, for beef sold at a premium, bringing a prosperity that rivaled the 1880's. In addition, there was a strong market for horses and mules, for in that conflict the army moved largely on genuine horsepower.

For those Arizonans who stayed home during the conflict, there was much to be done on farm, ranch, and mine, for industry was not yet a significant factor in the state's economy. Arizona, along with other states, had its Council of Defense, a branch of the National Council of Defense. This agency co-ordinated the selling of Liberty Bonds and secured support for the Red Cross. Patriotic feeling ran so high that in Phoenix one man who was suspected of not buying Liberty Bonds was smeared with yellow paint. Arizona also had its branch of the food administration which urged the conservation of food through such devices as "Wheatless" and "Meatless" days, and by advocating the growing of home vegetable gardens.

Arizona's young men were more directly involved in the war. Under terms of the Selective Service Act, the draft, 40,517 men were registered, of whom 15,283 were aliens and therefore not subject to call. Almost half the remaining men—totaling 11,410—became members of the armed forces: 8,113 in the National Guard, 1,854 in the Army, 1,269 in the Navy, and 147 in the Marine Corps. Of that number 321 died in service. The most famous Arizonan in that war was Frank Luke, Jr., the "Arizona Baloon Buster." This twenty-one-year-old pilot shot down twenty-one enemy aircraft in just thirty-nine days of combat before he was forced down behind German lines. Rather than surrender he died firing at the German soldiers who had come to capture him. He was awarded the Congressional Medal of Honor for his exploits, and his statue now stands on the state capitol grounds. Luke Field, an Air Force base near Phoenix, also commemorates his exploits.

Following the war many veterans came to Arizona to recover in its dry climate from the lung injuries they had sustained in Europe, where the Germans had used poison gas. In 1927, Congress authorized the building of a veterans' hospital in Tucson to serve them, the first of a number of such institutions in Arizona. That same year the Eighth Legislature granted veterans an exemption from state taxes in recognition of their contributions.

During the 1920's, Arizona, along with the rest of the country, was undergoing the "Noble Experiment" of prohibition. Luckily, Mexico was close enough for most Arizonans who wanted a drink to get it, and the cities were too small to attract organized bootlegging operations. Arizonans also entered the orgy of speculation associated with the stock market during that era, with some citizens actually getting rich at it. Of more long-range benefit to the state during this postwar period was the growth of tourism. Some working ranches had been taking in a few paying guests previous to the war, but afterward came the "dude ranches"—actually resorts in a ranch setting. Castle Hot Springs, a resort established in 1896 northwest of Phoenix, was the first hotel built to serve winter visitors. Others soon followed, such as the San Marcos Hotel in Chandler and the Arizona Inn at Tucson. The federal government aided the growth of tourism by its creation of parks, such as Grand Canyon National Park and the Petrified Forest National Monument, to which large numbers of visitors came.

The depression which began in 1929 and ended with the coming of World War II brought great distress to Arizona. Mines closed as the price of copper dropped to 5½¢ per pound, and many of the unemployed workers went into independent prospecting. Since the price of gold increased during the depression, these men opened old digs and hunted for new strikes. Farm workers were not so hard pressed, and the acreage under cultivation actually increased during these years, although wages were distressingly low. For the young there were Civilian Conservation Corps (CCC) camps in the mountains and the National Forests, while unemployed adults took jobs with the Works Progress Administration (WPA). Still many of the poor had to be fed from public kitchens, and Governor Rawghlie Stanford later would comment that rarely did he not look out and see one or more poor families camped on the lawn of the governor's mansion.

The approach of war restored prosperity to Arizona. Even before American entry into the conflict known as World War II, the federal government began constructing air training bases in the state: Luke Field near Phoenix, Davis-Monthan Field at Tucson, and Williams Field near Chandler. After the war began, the fear of a Japanese bombardment of the Pacific Coast—or even an actual invasion—led Washington war planners deliberately to encourage the establishment of industry in Arizona. The state was near Pacific ports, it had good weather almost all year, and it had an almost unlimited supply of labor available from Mexico. As a result, the state saw its first industrial boom. Consolidated Vultee established a plant at Tucson; the Garrett Corporation built its AiResearch plant at Phoenix Sky Harbor airport; the Allison Steel Company built portable bridges at Phoenix; the Aluminum Company of America built a huge extrusion plant at the same city; Goodyear Aircraft manufactured plane parts and balloons at Litchfield Park, adjacent to a naval air facility; while parts for tanks and airplanes were fabricated by subcontractors in a dozen towns and cities. Federal statistics show the result: in 1940 the gross income from manufacturing in Arizona was $17,000,000, while in 1945 the figure stood at $85,000,000.

Arizona became a huge training ground for troops of the army and air force during the conflict. In addition to the air bases already constructed, others were quickly readied: Marana and Ryan fields near Tucson, Thunderbird Field at Phoenix, and Falcon Field at Mesa. Gunnery training was conducted at Kingman; historic Fort Huachuca was used to train Negro soldiers, while Camp Horn near Wickenburg and Camp Hyder near Yuma were centers for training 200,000 soldiers in desert warfare. In addition, there were several prisoner-of-war camps for Germans and Italians in the state, and the Japanese-Americans (Nisei) from California were interned at several locations in Arizona. In fact, Poston (north of Yuma) became the third most populous city in the state for a time because of the Nisei there.

To the war itself Arizona sent approximately thirty thousand of its young men, who served with honor and distinction in all branches of the service and in all theaters of operations. Among these were the famed "Bushmasters" of the Arizona National Guard. One Arizonan, Silvestre S. Herrera, received the Medal of Honor, while a Pima Indian, Ira Hayes, was among the Marines who raised the flag at Iwo Jima.

During this conflict, Arizonans became familiar with rationing stamps for the purchase of gasoline, meat, sugar, coffee, shoes, automobile parts, tires, and many other items. They participated in scrap iron drives, and scoured junk heaps and trash dumps. They grew "victory gardens" to conserve food, and they took part in war bond drives. Yet at the same time they prospered, for the price of cotton, copper, and cattle soared. In more personal terms, this prosperity can be seen in Yuma. John Huber had opened a jewelry store there in the 1930's with modest success. With the war, some fifty thousand soldiers suddenly were stationed nearby, and overnight his business became spectacular. Anything on the shelves would sell, for he was in a business that attracted the soldiers. Business became so fantastic, in fact, that he had to post a guard at the front door and let in only a few customers at a time.

In Arizona the end of the war did mean the loss of many industrial jobs and a substantial loss of population. Industrial output fell from $85,000,000 in 1945 to

$53,000,000 in 1946. Yet for every war worker who left, there were more who stayed, and many veterans of the armed forces who had received their first glimpse of the Southwest at Arizona military camps returned to the state either to recuperate from war wounds, to go to school on the G.I. Bill, or to start businesses. The influx of population led to a booming construction industry, the growth of retail trade establishments, and a healthy economy in general. Some war plants were closed, but only temporarily, and the industries that remained helped attract other industries to the state. The Aluminum Company of America (Alcoa) plant at Phoenix was acquired by Reynolds Aluminum Corporation. AiResearch, which closed in 1946, was reopened in 1951 during the Korean War. Motorola, a major manufacturer of radio, television, and electronic parts, established a plant in Phoenix soon after the war ended. Soon other major electronic firms came to the state, such as General Electric, now a major employer in the state. The copper mining companies found that the end of the war had brought more, not less, demand for their product.

The war—and another development, air conditioning—had changed the face of Arizona. Because of the extreme heat in Arizona during the summer months, most wealthy citizens had fled to California in June, July, and August. Electric fans, introduced shortly after the turn of the twentieth century, did little but stir the hot air. Then, in 1934, came the evaporative cooler, known for years as the "Arizona Cooler." This device consisted of a low-speed electric exhaust fan mounted inside a cabinet, the sides of which were excelsior pads; water was kept running through the excelsior, and the moist air blown out by the fan cooled through evaporation. A. J. Eddy of Yuma generally is credited with the invention of this boon, which changed the pattern of life in the state. After its invention very few people found it necessary to leave during the summer months. Businesses, which previously had expected to lose money during the summer, suddenly found themselves making a profit. This boom in evaporative coolers stimulated the development of refrigerated cooling devices, for it showed that the rigors of desert heat could be mitigated and that people would gladly buy coolers.

The effects of the war and of air conditioning can be readily seen in population figures. Just prior to statehood, in 1910, Arizona had 294,353 residents. By 1920 the figure had jumped to 334,162, a 63 per cent gain. In 1930 there were 435,573 residents, a 30 per cent gain in the decade, while ten years later (1940) there were 499,261 people in the state, only a 15 per cent increase—the smallest percentage gain in the century. Between 1940 and 1950, however, the population jumped to 749,587, a 50 per cent gain in population.

This growth continued into the 1960's. By the start of that decade the census showed there were 1,302,161, a spectacular jump of some 75 per cent. Manufacturing had forged ahead of mining as the largest single source of income in the state; output from this source reached $1,000,000,000 in 1964. A spokesman for the Valley National Bank, which has been conducting research on the state's growth for three decades, declared, "Arizona's recent growth in manufacturing has been the most dynamic in the nation"—perhaps an understatement. Since the end of World War II, the state had grown 111 per cent in population; 156 per cent in non-agricultural employment, 296 per cent in income, and ranked first nationally in production of copper, second in silver, third in gold, and fifth in lead. Even the farmers have participated in this boom, although only slightly more than 2 per cent of the state is under cultivation. Agricultural income has jumped 167 per cent, while in 1965, for the seventeenth consecutive year, Arizona farmers led the nation in net income. That year they realized an average $21,423 net income per farm, compared with the national average of $4,604.

Nor is the end yet in sight. The United States Bureau of the Census released figures in 1970 showing the population to be 1,752,122. The metropolitan area of Phoenix is nearing the 1,000,000 mark, while Tucson trails behind, second, at 350,000. Industrial growth continues at a fast pace, surpassing $1,300,000,000 in value by 1966. Mining that year was worth over $600,000,000; agriculture was third at $450,000,000; and tourism was fourth at $425,000,000. Tentative figures for subsequent years show steady growth in all areas—and indicate an even richer future.

A number of touches of the old, free, romantic, adventurous frontier days still remain in Arizona despite its growth. Cowboys, Indians, "desert rats," ghost towns, abandoned army posts, lost mines, and incomparable natural wonders such as the Grand Canyon, the Petrified Forest National Monument, and desert scenery attract a stream of visitors to enjoy and marvel at the state and its wonders. They come as tourists, as winter visitors, and as convention-goers—and always some who come to visit stay to become residents. More and more industries are attracted to move plants to the state because of the welcome climate for business; by the strong educational facilities offered by the three state universities, the county junior college system, and the public schools; and by the avid response of employees who want to move to Arizona.

As Arizona turns toward a glowing future, it rests on a rich foundation of history. The state has problems, difficult ones, without doubt. For example, its tax base is small because 44 per cent of the land is owned by the federal government, 27 per cent by the Indians, and 13.5 per cent by the state, leaving only 15.5 per cent in private ownership subject to taxes. Its public educational facilities have been strained to capacity to hold the increasing number of students. Racial disturbances in Tucson and Phoenix in 1967–68 have shown that minority groups—Negroes and Latin Americans—want a place in the economic sun. And the Indians still on the reservations need aid and direction in order to join in the material and spiritual benefits of Arizona's dynamic society.

There still are problems to challenge those who wish to pioneer, to search for answers to grave questions. There are still mountains to climb, deserts to cross, rivers to ford, and hardships to be overcome—although of a different nature from those encountered by Arizona's first pioneers. Those early settlers—Indian, Spanish, Mexican, Oriental, Negro, and Anglo-American—came to the region with high hopes and dreams. They worked and they fought. They looked upon their children and hoped for something better for them. Some sought adventure and found it; some tried to start over again and failed; some hoped to get wealthy, but few did. Yet they fulfilled their destiny. They kept faith with their dreams. They transformed Arizona from a frontier into a vital part of the United States and helped mold the character of the nation. Present and future Arizonans can afford to do no less.

SUGGESTED READING LIST

The books listed below are not intended as a complete bibliography of Arizona history. Such a listing would fill several volumes and still be incomplete. For that reason I have divided my listing into four categories: bibliographies of Arizona, journals of interest to anyone studying Arizona's history, past histories of the state, and books which I feel are worthwhile reading about the state. Those books listed in the fourth category are meant merely as a starting point, a beginning, for the serious student of Arizona's long past; some are fiction, some are reminiscences, some are light reading, some are scholarly—but all should prove interesting and informative.

Bibliographies

Alliot, Hector. *Bibliography of Arizona*. Los Angeles, 1914.

Boyer, Mary. *Arizona in Literature*. Glendale, 1934.

Goodman, David M. *Arizona Odyssey: Bibliographic Adventures in Nineteenth-Century Magazines*. Tempe, 1970.

Lutrell, Estelle. *Bibliography of Arizona*. Tucson, 1916.

Munk, Joseph A. *A Bibliography of Arizona*. Los Angeles, 1900, 1914.

Powell, Donald M. *An Arizona Gathering*. Tucson, 1960.

Wagner, Henry R. *The Spanish Southwest, 1542–1794*. 2 vols. Albuquerque, 1937.

Wallace, Andrew (ed.). *Sources and Readings in Arizona History*. Tucson, 1965.

Journals

Arizona and the West. Tucson: The University of Arizona.

Arizona Highways. Phoenix: 2039 W. Lewis Avenue.

The Journal of Arizona History. Tucson: 949 East 2nd Street (free to members of the Arizona Pioneers' Historical Society).

State Histories

Bancroft, Hubert H. *History of Arizona and New Mexico, 1530–1888*. San Francisco, 1889, and reprint.

Cross, Jack L. (ed.). *Arizona, Its Land and Resources*. Tucson, 1960.

Elliott, Wallace W. (ed.). *History of Arizona Territory*. San Francisco, 1884, and reprint.

Farish, Thomas E. *History of Arizona*. 8 vols. San Francisco, 1914–18.

Goff, John S. *Arizona Civilization*. Phoenix, 1968.

McClintock, James H. *Arizona: Prehistoric, Aboriginal, Pioneer, Modern*. 3 vols. Chicago, 1916.

Miller, Joseph (ed.). *Arizona: A Guide to the Grand Canyon State*. New York, 1966.

Paré, Madeline F., and Fireman, Bert M. *Arizona Pageant*. Phoenix, 1965.

Peck, Ann M. *The March of Arizona History*. Tucson, 1962.

Peplow, Edward H. (ed.). *History of Arizona*. 3 vols. Phoenix, 1958.

Sloan, Richard E., and Ward R. Adams, *History of Arizona*. 4 vols. Phoenix, 1930.

Wyllys, Rufus K. *Arizona: The History of a Frontier State*. Phoenix, 1950.

General Readings

Arnold, Elliott. *Blood Brother*. New York, 1947, and reprints.

Arnold, Oren. *Arizona Under the Sun*. Freeport, Maine, 1968.

Arrowsmith, Rex. *Mines of the Old Southwest*. Santa Fe, 1963.

Baldwin, Gordon. *The Warrior Apaches*. Tucson, 1966.

Bartlett, John R. *Personal Narrative* . . . . 2 vols. New York, 1854, and reprint.

Barnes, Will C. *Arizona Place Names*. Tucson, 1935, and reprint.

Bolton, Herbert E. *Coronado: Knight of Pueblos and Plains*. Albuquerque, 1949, and reprint.

———. (ed.). *Kino's Historical Memoir of Pimería Alta*. 2 vols. Cleveland, 1919.

———. (ed.). *Spanish Exploration in the Southwest, 1542–1706*. New York, 1908, and reprint.

Bonsal, Stephen. *Edward Fitzgerald Beale.* New York, 1912.

Bourke, John G. *On the Border with Crook.* New York, 1891, and reprint.

Bourne, Eulalia. *Woman in Levi's.* Tucson, 1967.

Brinckerhoff, Sidney B., and Odie B. Faulk. *Lancers for the King.* Phoenix, 1965.

Cather, Willa. *Death Comes for the Archbishop.* New York, 1927, and reprint.

Clarke, Dwight L. *Stephen Watts Kearny: Soldier of the West.* Norman, 1961.

Cleland, Robert G. *A History of Phelps-Dodge, 1834–1950.* New York, 1952.

Conner, Daniel E. *Joseph Reddeford Walker and the Arizona Adventure.* Norman, 1956.

Cooke, Philip St. George. *The Conquest of New Mexico and California.* New York, 1878, and reprint.

Cosulich, Bernice. *Tucson, 1692–1900.* Tucson, 1953.

Dobie, J. Frank. *Apache Gold and Yaqui Silver.* Boston, 1939.

Erwin, Allen A. *The Southwest of John Horton Slaughter.* Glendale, 1965.

Faulk, Odie B. *The Geronimo Campaign.* New York, 1969.

———. *Too Far North—Too Far South.* Los Angeles, 1967.

Forbes, Jack D. *Apache, Navajo, and Spaniard.* Norman, 1960.

———. *Warriors of the Colorado.* Norman, 1965.

Forrest, Earle R. *Arizona's Dark and Bloody Ground.* Caldwell, Idaho, 1936.

———. *With a Camera in Old Navaholand.* Norman, 1970.

Furniss, Norman F. *The Mormon Conflict, 1850–1859.* New Haven, 1966.

Garber, Paul N. *The Gadsden Treaty*. Philadelphia, 1923, and reprint.

Gressinger, A. W. *Charles D. Poston: Sunland Seer*. Globe, Arizona, 1961.

Gustafson, A. M. (ed.). *John Spring's Arizona*. Tucson, 1964.

Hafen, LeRoy R. *The Overland Mail, 1849–1869*. Cleveland, 1926.

Hagan, William T. *Indian Police and Judges*. New Haven, 1966.

Haley, J. Evetts. *Jeff Milton: A Good Man with a Gun*. Norman, 1948.

Hall, Martin H. *Sibley's New Mexico Campaign*. Austin, 1960.

Hallenbeck, Cleve. *The Journey of Fray Marcos de Niza*. Dallas, 1949.

Hamilton, Patrick. *The Resources of Arizona*. San Francisco, 1881, 1884, and reprint.

Hammond, George P., and Agapito, Rey. *Don Juan de Oñate*. Albuquerque, 1953.

Henson, Pauline. *Founding a Wilderness Capital: Prescott, A. T.* Flagstaff, 1965.

Herner, Charles. *Arizona's Rough Riders*. Tucson, 1970.

Hodge, Hiram C. *Arizona As It Was*. New York, 1877, and reprint.

Horgan, Paul. *A Distant Trumpet*. New York, 1963.

Hunt, Aurora. *Major General James Henry Carleton, 1814–1873*. Glendale, 1958.

Johnson, Virginia W. *The Unregimented General: A Biography of Nelson A. Miles*. Boston, 1962.

Joralemon, Ira B. *Romantic Copper: Its Lure and Lore*. New York, 1935.

Kessell, John. *Guevavi: A Jesuit Mission in Arizona.* Tucson, 1970.

Leckie, William H. *The Buffalo Soldiers.* Norman, 1967.

Lockwood, Francis C. *Pioneer Days in Arizona.* New York, 1932.

———. *Pioneer Portraits.* Tucson, 1968.

Mann, Dean E. *The Politics of Water in Arizona.* Tucson, 1963.

Marcosson, Isaac F. *Anaconda.* New York, 1957.

Marshall, James. *Santa Fe: The Railroad that Built an Empire.* New York, 1945.

Myers, John M. *The Last Chance: Tombstone's Early Years.* New York, 1950.

Nevins, Allan. *Frémont: Pathmaker of the West.* New York, 1955.

Ormsby, Waterman L. *The Butterfield Overland Mail.* San Marino, California, 1942.

Pattie, James O. *Personal Narrative* . . . . Available in many editions.

Poston, Charles D. *Apache Land.* San Francisco, 1878.

———. *Building a State in Apache Land.* Tempe, Arizona, 1963.

Powell, Donald M. *The Peralta Grant.* Norman, 1960.

Quebbeman, Francis E. *Medicine in Territorial Arizona.* Phoenix, 1966.

Roca, Paul M. *Paths of the Padres Through Sonora.* Tucson, 1967.

Sacks, B. *Be It Enacted: The Creation of the Territory of Arizona.* Phoenix, 1964.

Salpointe, John B. *Soldiers of the Cross.* Banning, California, 1898, and reprint.

Schellie, Don. *Vast Domain of Blood: the Story of the Camp Grant Massacre.* Los Angeles, 1968.

Sherman, James E. and Barbara H. *Ghost Towns of Arizona*. Norman, 1969.

Schmitt, Martin F. (ed.). *General George Crook: His Autobiography*. Norman, 1946.

Smalley, George H. *My Adventures in Arizona*. Tucson, 1966.

Smith, Cornelius C., Jr. *William Saunders Oury*. Tucson, 1967.

Smith, Fay, John Kessell, and Francis Fox. *Father Kino in Arizona*. Phoenix, 1966.

Spicer, Edward H. *Cycles of Conquest*. Tucson, 1962.

Steward, George R. *John Phoenix, Esq., the Veritable Squibob*. New York, 1935.

Summerhayes, Martha. *Vanished Arizona*. New York, 1908, and reprint.

Terrell, John U. *War for the Colorado River*. 2 vols. Glendale, 1966.

Thrapp, Dan L. *Al Sieber, Chief of Scouts*. Norman, 1964.
———. *The Conquest of Apacheria*. Norman, 1967.

Towne, Charles W., and Edward N. Wentworth. *Shepherd's Empire*. Norman, 1945.

Udall, David K., and Pearl U. Nelson. *Arizona Pioneer Mormon*. Tucson, 1959.

Wellman, Paul I. *Broncho Apache*. New York, 1936.

Wilson, Neill C. *Southern Pacific: the Roaring Story of a Fighting Railroad*. New York, 1952.

Woodward, Arthur. *Feud on the Colorado*. Los Angeles, 1955.

Young, Otis E., Jr. *How They Dug the Gold*. Tucson, 1966.

———. *The West of Philip St. George Cooke, 1809–1895*. Glendale, 1955.

INDEX